BRENNY

W9-CUF-092

Medical Terminology

Medical Terminology

A PROGRAMED TEXT

GENEVIEVE LOVE SMITH

Coordinator of Programing
Point Park College

PHYLLIS E. DAVIS

Dean of the college
Point Park College
Pittsburgh, Pennsylvania

Second Edition

JOHN WILEY & SONS, INC.
New York · London · Sydney

Copyright © 1963, 1967 by John Wiley & Sons, Inc.

All Rights Reserved

This book or any part thereof must not be reproduced in
any form without the written permission of the publisher.

18 19 20

Library of Congress Catalog Card Number: 66-30383
Printed in the United States of America

ISBN 0 471 80196 8

Preface

MEDICAL TERMINOLOGY: a programed text, published in 1963, was widely used and gratifyingly well received, so we decided to incorporate, in a new edition, improvements suggested by users and justified by our further experience and testing. The change in format is dramatic; but it is not the only change that has been made. We have received helpful criticism as well as encouragement from teachers in other schools. We have gathered more data here at Point Park College. These, plus student questions and comment, provide the basis for this revision.

The original "To The Teacher" has been retained because we hope that new users will find it as valid and helpful as many teachers have indicated it to be. The material that was formerly called the "Introduction" is vital in understanding the word-building process, so it has been incorporated into the main body of the text in the first 87 frames. These frames should be considered one assignment. The part of this assignment that could be called "the anatomy of the word" has been considerably reworked in order to clarify two areas. If students forget this part, as many do later in the course, they should be reminded to rework frames 29 through 67. It is our opinion that the reason students forget the word-building system in its entirety is that word-building becomes automatic to them quite early in the learning process.

Throughout the body of the text, frames have been reworked on the basis of feedback. Since experience revealed that students were reluctant to remove the colored panels for reference use, we incorporated these units into the body of the text. The review sheets have been left at the end of the textual material because there is no reason why they should be removed from the book.

In order to increase the versatility of this program, a second glossary has been prepared containing word parts that the student has not yet met. These words are useful medically and can be learned easily by the word-building system. These word parts along with one suggestion for their use are in Appendix C. This appendix should be of help to teachers who have more time for the teaching of medical terminology than that shown in the suggested assignment page. There are also those wonderful students who are intellectually curious; they will enjoy Appendix C. A third use for this glossary of new word parts is to enrich the course for the exceptionally rapid learner. Appendix B remains a glossary of word parts that the student has already used. It refers the student to the frame in which the word part was introduced. We assume that if a student wants to look up a particular word he will use his dictionary.

The suggested assignments have been changed and the change tested with one class of students. The change, as reflected in students' grades, appears to have no effect on learning. We made this change for two reasons. First, assignment of material between tests is better distributed. Second, as most teachers know, "administrative considerations" or a holiday can cause the loss of one, two, or even three class hours in any given term. The assignments as now set up compensate for these possible conditions. If no time is lost, however, Appendix C can be used to help the student learn how to continue building his professional vocabulary.

One suggestion made by some teachers who use this text is to classify the word parts under anatomical systems. We have not made this change because so many medical word parts cannot be classified in this manner. All prefixes and suffixes cut across anatomical systems; so do many combining forms (e. g., patho, plasto, micro, tropho, etc.). An actual count showed many more word parts that could be used with several systems than those which could be classified under a single anatomical system. Since most students using this text will also have a course in anatomy, anatomical terms have received little emphasis. They have been carefully introduced at two points late in the book and have been presented in such a manner that all of the student's knowledge of anatomical terminology is transferred to the building of medical words.

Even before the publication of the original text in 1963, we were working to acquire valid, uncontaminated information on retention of material over a period of time. After using 14 classes of students to develop two forms of a test that sampled the entire course, we were confident that we had valid tests for measuring retention over a period of time. On December 23, 1965, Form A was administered to 33 students as a terminal test. On January 12, 1966, Form B was administered to these same students as a time-lapse test. The students were in no way expecting further testing on a course already finished. The time lapse was three weeks. The assumption was made that in these three weeks, which embraced the Christmas holiday and registration for the new trimester, little if any contamination of results was likely. A score of 50 points was possible on both Form A and Form B of the test. On the terminal test (December 23) the mean score was 46.12. On the time-lapse test (January 12) the mean score was 44.03. These scores exposed to a T-test showed no significant difference.

Since the number of students available for the experiment was relatively small (**N** = 33) a correlation of individual scores on both tests was run. Using the Pearson product–moment coefficient of correlation, the result obtained was **r** = .687. We were more than satisfied with the above findings.

We wish to express our appreciation for statistical work to Mrs. Rainette Fu of our Computer Center. We also want to acknowledge the long hours and creative suggestions of Miss Judy Szafranski, the secretary who worked on this revision.

Genevieve Love Smith
Phyllis E. Davis

Pittsburgh, Pennsylvania
January 1967

Acknowledgments

We wish to express special gratitude to the administration of Point Park College for complete backing in this project.

Without the encouragement and faith of Dr. Dorothy C. Finkelhor, President of Point Park College, the program in medical terminology could never have been constructed.

The help of Mr. Arthur Blum, Executive Vice-President of the college, was essential. His understanding of the enormity of the project was a source of encouragement to the programer.

Without the financial backing of the college's administration, there could have been no program. The assumption of such a risk, based on faith alone, is something that can never be adequately acknowledged.

Our appreciation is expressed to Dr. L. Herbert Finkelhor for his sustained interest throughout the entire project. Our thanks also go to Miss Margaret Jones, Miss Andrea Hamilton, and Miss Carol Frank for help above and beyond the call of ordinary secretarial duties.

G. L. S.
P. E. D.

For the Reader's Information

Objectives of the Program

Upon the completion of this text, the student will respond by:
1. building literally thousands of medical words from Greek and Latin prefixes, suffixes, word roots, and combining forms.
2. recognizing medical words from the Greek and Latin parts.
3. spelling medical words correctly.
4. using a medical dictionary intelligently.

Population Intended

1. Those studying in the field of medicine or the paramedical fields (future nurses, medical secretaries, medical technologists, medical librarians, veterinarians, medical assistants, etc.).
2. Graduates working in the paramedical fields who feel the need to renew or increase their vocabulary.
3. People in the world of business who have frequent contact with the world of medicine.
4. Members of the Armed Services working in a medically related capacity.

Prerequisites

High school education

Pretests

None. It is assumed that pretests would be of no value with so technical a vocabulary.

To The Teacher

This text was designed to be used for a 30-hour course in medical terminology. It was designed for the post-high school student who is going into the field of medicine or one of the professions relating to medicine. It is useful for anyone wanting a background in the language of medicine.

Although this text can be used completely auto-instructionally, it is best used in a course that meets regularly with an instructor. At Point Park College, where it was developed, it is used with medical secretarial students and Associate-in-Science-degree nursing students. The frames (see p. xvii) are assigned as homework for a 30-hour, two-credit course. Since some students will require more drill and review than others, 35 review sheets are included. It is upon the individual student that the initiative for the use of these review sheets is placed. The average student will need to work about two hours outside of class for every 50-minute class period. (There is one exceptional student on record who averaged only 35 minutes per assignment and maintained a straight-A grade on the eight criterion tests.)

It may be of interest to the reader to know that medical terminology has been taught at Point Park College successfully for seventeen years. A reduction in class time for the course from 120 hours to 30 hours stimulated the development of the program. The tests which form the criteria for the course are the same type as have always been given. Statistical evidence obtained from past grades and the grades of the eight classes which used the program for homework has shown that there has been no decline in accomplishment. Nor has there been any significant change in the average age of our students or their mental ability as determined by the Otis Form A for high schools and colleges.

In class time we have followed this procedure: At the beginning of the class period, 10 to 15 minutes are used in pronouncing the words. This drill assures that all students are pronouncing correctly and learning accent shifts with such word parts as "pathy," "lysis," and "clysis." * Next, the students are encouraged to ask any questions that the program has suggested to them. The program is so constructed that the skillful teacher will usually have the opportunity to spend the rest of the class period answering questions and guiding questions in the direction that he or she desires. It takes two or three class sessions before the ability to question is developed properly in the student. During these first two or three sessions, medical ethics and the need for exactness and care in the medical field are discussed. The Hippocratic oath is read and discussed. Some stories from the instructor's experience illustrating this material are included. The practice of reading medical journals rather than popular periodicals (such as those featuring "the disease of the month") is encouraged. Students are told, though they rarely seem to comprehend, that neither they nor the instructor is trained in diagnosis.

At this point the students are sufficiently far into the program for a vocabulary to be built which will form a framework for discussion of the more important diseases, diagnostic terms, etc., that are introduced with the programed homework. An opaque projector is used to show anatomical drawings and pictures of disease. Library assignments are made first to anatomical drawings† and later to such enrichment material as is available and suitable to the ability of the group. Occasionally there is an outstanding group that cannot only take more but wants more. To a group like this, additional combining forms and prefixes may be given. Also with these students more synthesis between the Greek and Latin word-parts as they relate to ordinary English usage can be undertaken. For the average class and the average college student, however, there is quite enough material in the programed text for a 30-hour course. All tests are limited to words programed and responded to.

In deciding how best to incorporate this program into his own teaching plans, the instructor should, as with any program, go through a considerable part of the material, starting with the first frame and continuing until he sees the system underlying it. As he continues into the program, he will find that there is a considerable element of discovery built into the frames themselves. This discovery seems to be a source of motivation to the student.

There is another thing he will notice which may seem odd at first. The program starts with the unfamiliar and waits until two-thirds of

---

*The dictionary used in the creation of this program was Taber's Cyclopedic Medical Dictionary (F. A. Davis Company, Philadelphia, Pennsylvania.) The program can be used successfully with other medical dictionaries, however, and was so used on several occasions in the process of developing the program.

†These drawings by Dr. Frank H. Netter are in the CIBA Collection of Medical Illustrations and in Clinical Symposia, both of which are published by CIBA Pharmaceutical Products Company, Summit, New Jersey.

the way through the course to introduce something familiar (i.e., the bones of the body). There is a double reason for this procedure. First, most students taking this course will be taking it simultaneously with anatomy. The bone section in the program is held up until students have learned the bones of the body. Then, with a relatively few examples, the students discover how to find their own combining forms for the already familiar. When learned at this time, this knowledge usually carries across all their anatomical terms and teaches transfer and synthesis. The second reason for going from the unfamiliar to the familiar rests on some of the psychological principles involved with programing. The further one goes into a vocabulary-building course, the more repetition is necessary for competent usage.

It may seem that some useless words have been programed. This is occasionally true. It was necessary, at times, in order to elicit a sufficient number of responses from the student to a new word part, the use of which depended on those word parts he had already learned. These words of lesser importance are not included in the eight criterion tests.

A concurrent course in anatomy has already been mentioned. In order for the program to be effective, anatomy is helpful but not necessary. For experimental purposes, the program was worked by a student who had no knowledge of anatomy and had no high school biology. She averaged 95.6% as a final grade on the eight tests. She did the work completely on her own with no class sessions whatever and averaged two-and-one-half hours study time per assignment.

For the reader interested in the results obtained by this program's use at Point Park College, the following comparisons may be of moment. The data are based on a series of eight criterion tests* which measured word-building, word-recognition from word-parts, and spelling. The classes involved were that of 1960, in which the verbal material was taught by lecture, text, and drill; and those of 1961 and 1962 in which this material was taught by the program. The 1960 class had the 120 hour course, while the 1961 and 1962 classes had a course of only 30-hour duration. The information regarding dropouts (on page xvi) is most interesting:

1960			1961			1962				
A	37	37%	A	26	30.0%	A	16	26.7%	A	95–100
B	33	33%	B	32	37.0%	B	27	45.0%	B	88–94
C	20	20%	C	16	18.4%	C	13	21.7%	C	80–87
D	9	9%	D	10	11.5%	D	1	1.7%	D	70–79
F	4	4%	F	3	3.4%	F	3	5.0%	F	Below 70
	103			87			60			

*Teachers may obtain these tests plus a final examination by writing to the publisher.

Dropouts: 1960—11
                8 due to failing Medical Terminology
                3 due to other causes
      1961— 1 reason not related to course
      1962— 0

The eight failing dropouts in 1960 are not included in the statistics because they did not finish the course.

We will appreciate comments and suggestions from teachers, students, and self-teachers who have used this program.

G. L. S.
P. E. D.

Contents

APPENDICES

Medical Terminology

How to Work the Program

1

Directions: Cover the answer column with a folded piece of paper.

A frame is a piece of information plus a blank (_____) in which you write. All this material following the number 1 is a _____.

frame
Now go on to Frame 2

Check your answer by sliding down your cover paper.

2

By checking your answer immediately, you know whether or not you are right. This immediate knowledge helps you to learn only what is _____ _____ (right/wrong).

right
Now go on to Frame 3

Check your answer by sliding down your cover paper.

3

A program is a way of learning that tells you immediately when you are right. When you work a series of frames and are certain that you are right, you are learning from a _____.

program

Check your answer by sliding down your cover paper.

4

By means of a program, you can also learn at your own speed. Learning at your own speed and having immediate knowledge that you are learning correctly are both advantages of a

program

_____.

Always check your answers immediately.

5

You will learn medical terminology from a program. Class will be more interesting because you will come prepared for it having worked your

program

_____.

1

6

When you see (_____), your answer will need only one word. In the sentence, "This is a program in _____ terminology," you know to use _____ word.

medical
one

7

This single blank (_____) contains a clue. It is proportional to the length of the word needed. This short blank (_____) means one short word. The long blank (_____) means one _____ word.

long

8

Whenever you see a blank space (_____), you know to write _____ (one/more than one) word. You also know something about the _____ (length/complexity) of the word.

one

length

9

Whenever you see a star blank (*_____), your answer will require more than one word. In the sentence, "This is a programed course in *____ _____," your answer requires *_____.

medical terminology
more than one word

10

In (*_____) there is no clue to the length of the words or how many words. The important thing to remember is that (*_____) means *_____.

more than one word

11

When you see a double-star blank (**_____ _____) use your own words. In the sentence, "I think a programed course in medical terminology will be **_____," you are expected to **_____.

anything from interesting to dull (If you did not answer this one, it doesn't matter.) use own words

12

In the sentence, "I want to go to college because (**_____)," you are free to **_____.

use own words

13

Now summarize what you have learned so far:

one

(_____) means _____word

(_____) gives a clue about the _____

length
more than one

_____ of the word.

(*_____) means *_____

use own

_____ word.

(**_____) means **_____

_____ words.

14

The fact that you check your answer immediately is very important for efficient, accurate learning.

check the answer
immediately

Every time you fill a blank, you will **_____

_____.

15

When working a program, **never look ahead.** There are many reasons for this, but the important thing to learn now is

never look ahead

*_____.

16

You may always look back to find something you have forgotten. You will probably have to look back,

ahead

but never look _____.

17

If you make even one error, look back to see where you were wrong. Correct the error; then go on. You

back
never

must always look _____, but _____ look ahead.

18

Never let a wrong answer go uncorrected. Each time

correct

you make an error, you _____ it.

19

This is a new way of learning. **This is not a test.** Remember always, this is a way of

learning

_____.

20

Do not be ashamed of a mistake; this is **not** a test.

back
correct

If you make an error, simply look _____ to see where you were wrong; and then _____ _____ the error.

3

21

Summarize what you have learned about the mechanics of working a program:

one

more than one

(_____) means _____ word.
(*_____) means *_____
_____ word.

my own

(**_____) means **_____
_____ words.

22

Continue to summarize:

corrected

Any error must be _____.

back

You may always look _____.

ahead

Never look _____.

This is not a test. It is a way of

learning

_____.

23

information frame

The material to be learned in the first 87 frames is the most important part of the entire course. This teaches the **system** of word building you will use in Medical Terminology.

24

Since the material in the first 87 frames is so important, you will learn it thoroughly before you start to build medical words. Once you understand this

thoroughly, well, or anything that means this

material the rest is fun. Learn the first 87 frames **
_____

_____. (How?)

25

Medical Terminology is a course designed to teach a medical vocabulary. Physicians use a medical

vocabulary or terminology

_____.

26

Every field of knowledge has its own particular terminology. In the field of medicine, this is a med-

terminology or even vocabulary

ical _____.

27

In any field of knowledge, a special vocabulary is necessary to speak or write **exactly.** Physicians use a medical vocabulary to speak or write

exactly

_____.

4

The Word-Building System

28

Medicine has a large vocabulary, but you can learn much of it by word building. When you put words together from their parts, you are _____ building.

word

29

All words have a word root. Even ordinary, everyday words have a *_____.

word root

30

The word root is the foundation of a word. Trans/port, ex/port, im/port, and sup/port have port as their *_____.

word root

31

Suf/fix, pre/fix, af/fix, and fix/ation have fix as their *_____.

word root

32

The word root in tonsill/itis, tonsill/ectomy, and tonsill/ar is _____.

tonsill *TONSIL*

33

The foundation of the word is the *_____.

word root

34

Compound words can be formed when two word roots are used to build the word. Even in ordinary English, two word roots are used to form *_____.

compound words

35

Sometimes the two word roots are words. They still form a compound word. Short/hand is a *_____.

compound word

36

Short/change, short/wave, and short/stop are also

compound words

*_____.

37

Two or more word roots mean a word is a

compound word

*_____.

38

Form a compound word using the word roots, **under** and **age:** _____

underage

39

Form a compound word from the word roots, chicken and pox. _____

chickenpox

40

A combining form is a word root plus a vowel. In the word therm/o/meter, therm/o is the

combining form

*_____

41

In the word speed/o/meter, speed/o is the

combining form

*_____.

42

In the words micr/o/scope, micr/o/film, and micr/o/be, micr/o is the

combining form

*_____.

43

The combining form of word roots is also used to build compound words. The previous examples, therm/o/meter, speed/o/meter, micr/o/scope, and micr/o/film are

compound words

*_____.

44

Compound words can also be formed from a **combining form** and a whole **word**. Thermometer is a compound word built from a combining form and a word. In the word therm/o/meter:

    therm/o is the

combining form

    *_____.

word

    meter is the _____.

6

45

Build a compound word from the combining forms micr/o plus:

microscope scope _____ / _/ _____.

microfilm film _____ / _/ _____.

micrometer meter _____ / _/ _____.

46

Build a compound word from the combining form hydr/o plus:

hydroplane plane _____ / _/ _____.

hydrometer meter _____ / _/ _____.

hydrofoil foil _____ / _/ _____.

47

compound The words you built in frames 45 and 46 are _____ _____ words.

48

In medical terminology, compound words are usually built from a **combining form,** a **word root,** and an **ending.** In the word micr/o/scop/ic,

   micr/o is the combining form,

   scop   is the word root,

ending   ic   is the _____.

49

In the word therm/o/metr/ic,

   therm/o is the combining form,

word root   metr   is the *_____,

ending   ic   is the _____.

50

In the word electr/o/metr/ic,

combining form   electr/o is the *_____,

word root   metr   is the *_____,

ending   ic   is the _____.

51

Build a word from:

   the combining form electr/o,

   the word root   stat,

   the ending   ic.

electrostatic _____ / _/ _____ / _____

52

Build a word from:

the word root   chlor,
the combining form hydr/o,
the ending   ic.

hydrochloric

_____ / ___ / _____ / _____

53

Build a word from:

the ending   ide
the combining form hydr/o
the word root   chlor

hydrochloride

_____ / ___ / _____ / _____

54

If you missed either of the last two frames, rework the program starting with frame 48.

55

The ending that follows a word root is a suffix. You can change the meaning of a word by putting another part after it. This other part is a

suffix

_____.

56

The suffix **er** means **one who.** The word root, port (to carry), is changed by putting **er** after it. In the word port/er, **er** is a _____.

suffix

57

In the word read/able, able changes the meaning of read. **able** is a _____.

suffix

58

In the words plant/er, plant/ed, and plant/ing, the suffixes are _____, _____, _____.

er, ed, ing

59

A prefix is a word part that goes before a word. You can change the meaning of the word by putting another part before it. This other part is a

prefix

_____.

60

The prefix **ex** means from. The word root, port (to carry), is changed by putting **ex** in front of it. In the word ex/port, **ex** is a _____.

prefix

61

In the word dis/please, **dis** changes the meaning of please. **dis** is a _____.

prefix

62

In the words im/plant, sup/plant, and trans/plant, the prefixes are _____, _____, and _____.

im, sup, trans

63

Before learning more, review what you have learned. The foundation of a word is a
*_____.

word root

64

The word part that is placed before a word to change its meaning is a _____.

prefix

65

The word part that follows a word root is a
_____.

suffix

66

When a vowel is added to a word root, the word part that results is a
*_____.

combining form

67

When some form of two or more word roots is used to form a word, the word formed is called a *_____
_____.

compound word

How to Study Medical Terminology

68

This is a system of word building. There are exceptions to all systems. This system of word building also has _____.

exceptions

69

It is important to learn the system. It is impossible to memorize enough medical words! By using a few word parts, you can build thousands of words, if you know the _____.

system

70

Although there are exceptions to this system of word building, it is important to know the

_____.

system

information frame

71

There is a way of handling the few exceptions to this system of word building. When you write a new word and check your answer, you will usually find the pronunciation given. Pronounce the word **out loud** and listen to what you are saying.

72

Each new word should be pronounced **out loud** several times. This helps you to spot exceptions to the word-building _____.

system

73

Pronouncing **out loud** is not much good if you don't listen to what you are saying. Always pronounce new words **out loud** and _____ to what you are saying.

listen

74

Saying and listening will help you spot exceptions to the word-building _____.

system

75

Saying and **listening** will do much more for you. On the following drawing, find the parts of the brain used when saying and listening. (Refer to this drawing while working the next 8 frames.)

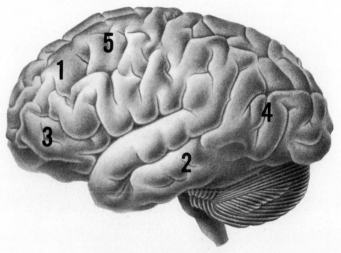

1. thinking area
2. hearing area
3. saying area
4. seeing area
5. writing area

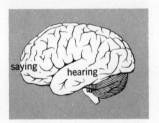

76

On this picture of the brain, label the parts that help you remember a word when you **say** it and **listen** to it.

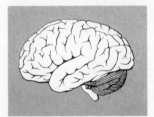

Do it

77

If you look at the word when you say it and hear it, you are using a third part of the brain to help you remember. Find the part of the brain that sees the word.

78

Label the parts of the brain that:
  say
  see
  hear

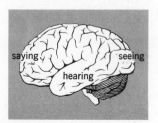

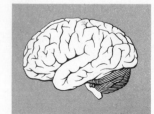

11

Do it

79

If you think of what you are saying, seeing, and hearing, you involve a fourth part of the brain in the memory process. Find this fourth part of the brain.

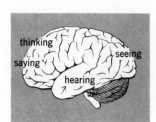

80

Label the parts of the brain that see, hear, say, and think.

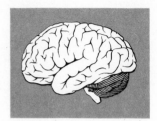

81

If you have four parts of the brain working for you at the same time, you will learn much faster. This is efficient learning. It makes sense to say a word, listen to it, look at it, and think about it in one operation.

82

say, think, see, hear, (or something that means this)

Each time you see this picture you will remember to ** _____

_____

_____ .

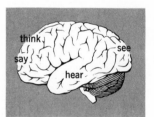

83

See how efficiently you are learning!

When you wrote the new word, you impressed it on a fifth part of the brain. Find this part of the brain on the large drawing.

84

In Appendix A there are several review sheets. You will be told when to work them and reminded to rework them. Don't worry about them now. Don't even look at them, because that would be looking

ahead

_____ .

85

Look at the picture in Frame 82.

You rework review sheets as soon as a word part stops **ringing in your ears.** This will be related to how well you did what the picture in frame 82 suggests.

think

86
Of course, anytime you work you should

_____ .

think

87
While building medical words, follow the method you have been using. If you find you are forgetting your word-building system, rework **Frames 29 through 65.**

You are now ready to start building medical words.

Medical Terminology

88

_____A____/B_____ means a word root and its combining form. **A** is the word root; **AB** is the combining form. In acr/o, acr is the *_____

word root

and acr/o is the

combining form

 *_____.

89

word root

In megal/o, megal is the *_____

and megal/o is the

combining form

  *_____.

90

word root

In dermat/o, dermat is the *_____

and dermat/o is the

combining form

  *_____.

91

acr/o
or
acr

Acr/o is used to build words that refer to the extremities. To refer to extremities, physicians use words containing _____ .

92

Acr/o is found in words concerning the extremities, which in the human body are the arms and legs. To build words about the arms use

acr/o

   _____/____ .

93

acr/o

To build words about the legs use _____/____ .

94

Acr/o any place in a word should make you think of the extremities. When you read a word containing acr or acr/o, you think of

extremities

_____.

14

95

In the word acr/o/paralysis (acroparalysis) acr/o refers to _____.

extremities

96

The words acr/o/megaly (acromegaly), acr/o/cyan/osis (acrocyanosis), and acr/o/dermat/itis (acrodermatitis) all refer to the

extremities

_____.

97

Megal/o means enlarged. Megal/o can also mean large. A word containing megal/o will mean something is ** _____.

large
big
enlarged

98

Acr/o/megal/y (acromegaly) means that the extremities are _____.

large, big, or enlarged

99

Acr/o/megal/y means enlargement of the extremities. The word that means a person has enlarged hands is _____.

acr/o/megal/y
acromegaly
ak ro meg' a li

100

Acromegaly can be a specific disorder of the body. Symptoms are enlargement of the bones of the hands and feet, as well as some of the bones of the head. A patient with these symptoms is said to have _____.

acromegaly

101

Occasionally you see a person with very large hands, feet, nose, and chin. His skin also has a coarse texture. He probably has

acromegaly

_____.

102

y is a suffix that makes a word a noun. Acromegaly is a _____.

noun

103

Dermat/o refers to the skin. When you see dermat or dermat/o, think immediately of _____.

skin

104

A dermat/o/logist (dermatologist) is a specialist in a field of medicine. He specializes in diseases of the _____.

skin

105

acr/o/dermat/itis
acrodermatitis
ak ro der ma ti' tis

Acr/o/dermat/itis (acrodermatitis) is a word that means inflammation of the skin of the extremities. A person with red, inflamed hands has

_____ .

106

acrodermatitis

Acrodermatitis could result from stepping in a patch of poison ivy. A person with red, inflamed feet has

_____ .

107

acrodermatitis

A simpler way to say that a patient is suffering from an inflammation of the hands, lower arms, feet, and legs is to say that he has

_____ .

108

inflammation

Remembering the word acrodermatitis which means inflammation of the skin of the extremities, draw a conclusion. **itis** is a suffix that means

_____ .

109

cyan/o
or
cyan

Cyan/o is used in words to mean blue or blueness. When a photographer wants to say something about how a film reproduces the color blue, he uses

_____ .

110

cyan

Acr/o/cyan/osis means blueness of the extremities. The part of the word that tells you that the color blue is involved is _____ .

111

acr/o/cyan/osis
acrocyanosis
ak ro si a no' sis

Acr/o/cyan/osis results from lack of oxygen. When the blood doesn't carry enough oxygen to the hands and feet, _____
results.

112

acrocyanosis

Acrocyanosis, or blueness of the extremities, is usually related to the amount of oxygen getting to the hands and feet. When the heart doesn't pump enough blood carrying oxygen, the patient exhibits

_____ .

113

When the lungs cannot get enough oxygen into the blood because of asthma, blueness of the extremities may result. This is another cause of

acrocyanosis

_____.

114

Acrocyanosis means

blueness of the
extremities

**_____.

115

osis is a suffix which makes a word a noun and means condition. To say a condition of blueness of the extremities, use the suffix _____.

osis

116

Acrocyanosis is a _____. (noun/verb)

noun

117

Paralysis is a word that means loss of movement. Form a compound word meaning paralysis of the extremities.

acr/o/paralysis
acroparalysis
ak ro pa ral' i sis

_____ / _____ / _____

118

Did you get it? Good. If not, restudy to see what was wrong. Now go on. Remember, dermat/o means _____.

skin

119

Dermat/itis means inflammation of the skin. The suffix that means inflammation is _____.

itis

120

Dermatitis immediately forms a picture of red skin. To say that the skin is inflamed, physicians use the word _____.

dermat/itis
dermatitis
der mat i' tis

121

Analyze the word dermat/itis. **Itis** means inflammation of the (dermat) _____.

skin

122

Dermat/osis means any skin condition. This word denotes an abnormal skin condition. The suffix that means condition is _____.

osis

123

osis: is a suffix
  forms a noun
  means condition
Build a word that means a condition of blueness.

cyan/osis
cyanosis
si an o' sis

_____ / _____

124

Build a word that means condition of the skin.

dermat/osis
dermatosis
der mat o' sis

_____ / _____

125

The Greek word, tomos, means **a piece cut off.**
From this word we have many combining forms
which refer to cutting: ec/tom/y (cut out), o/tom/y
(cut into), tome (an instrument that cuts).
This frame is just for fun, so write "tome."

tome

_____

126

Remember to associate **tom** (tome, ectomy, and
otomy) with cutting. A dermatome is an instrument

skin

that cuts _____ .

127

A dermatome is an instrument. When a physician
wants a thin slice of a patient's skin for examination under a microscope, he will ask for a

dermatome
der' ma/tōm

_____ .

128

Did you get it? If so, you are really learning medical
terminology. (This one is for free.)

129

Derm/o is another combining form for words referring to the skin. Cyan/o/derm/a (cyanoderma)

skin

means a blueish discoloration of the _____ .

130

Derma is a word itself. It is a noun meaning skin.
Cyan/o/derm/a is a compound word. It means

blue skin or
blueish discoloration
of the skin

**
_____

noun

and is a _____ .
    (noun/adjective)

18

131

Cyanoderma sometimes occurs when children swim too long in cold water. If a person has a blueish discoloration of the skin for any reason, he suffers from _____.

cyan/o/derm/a
cyanoderma
si an o der' ma

132

Leuk/o means white. There are many words in medicine that refer to white. To say something is white, use _____.

leuk/o
or
leuk

133

In the compound word leuk/o/derm/a, the part that means white is _____.

leuk or leuk/o

134

Leuk/o/derm/a means
            **
_____.

white skin,
abnormally white skin,
whiteness of the skin, etc.

135

Some people have much less color in their skin than is normal. Their skin is white. They have
_____ / _____ / _____ / _____.

leuk/o/derm/a
leukoderma
lu ko der' ma

136

Some people have white areas on their skin. Sometimes these white areas are called
_____ / _____ / _____ / _____.

leuk/o/derm/a

137

Cyt/o refers to cells. Cells are the smallest unit of life. To refer to this smallest part of a body that can live, _____ / _____ is used.

cyt/o

138

Cytology is the study of cells. The part of cyt/o/logy that means cells is _____ / _____.

cyt/o

139

There are several kinds of cells in blood. One kind is a leuk/o/cyte. A leukocyte is a white blood
_____.

cell

140

There are several kinds of leukocytes in the blood. When a physician wants to know how many leukocytes of all kinds there are, he will ask for a
_____ / _____ / _____ / _____ count.

leuk/o/cyt/e
leukocyte
lu' ko sīt

19

141

If a physician wants to know how many there are of one kind of leukocyte, he asks for a differential

leuk/o/cyt/e

_____ / _____ / _____ / _____ count.

142

Leuk/o/cyt/o/penia (leukocytopenia) means a decrease in white blood cells. The part of the word that means **decrease in** is _____ .

penia

143

Penia is the Greek word for poverty. The word that means **decrease in** or **not enough** white blood cells is

leuk/o/cyt/o/penia
leukocytopenia
lu ko sīt o pe' ni a

_____ / _____ / _____ / _____ / _____ .

144

If the body does not produce enough white blood cells, the patient suffers from

leukocytopenia

_____ .

145

Red blood cells are erythrocytes. If a patient lacks red blood cells, he suffers from

cyt/o/penia

_____ erythr /o/ _____ / _____ / _____ .

146

You have heard of leuk/em/ia, popularly called, "blood cancer." **ia** is a noun ending. **em** comes from a Greek word meaning, "blood." A noun meaning literally, "white blood," is

leuk/em/ia
leukemia
lu ke' mi a

_____ / _____ / _____ .

147

In leukemia, the blood is not really white. A symptom of this disease is the presence of too many leukocytes in the blood. This symptom was used to name the disease

leukemia

_____ / _____ / _____ .

148

In the word acr/o/megal/y, the word root for big or large is _____ .

megal

149

The combining form of megal is _____ / _____ .

megal/o

20

cardiamegaly

large heart
enlargement of
the heart

megal/o/cardi/a
megalocardia
meg a lo kar' di a

megalocardia

megalocardia

megalocardia

gastr

megal/o/gastr/ia
megalogastria
meg a lo gas' tri a

megalogastria

condition

150
Cardi/o is the combining form for words about the heart. Megal/o/cardi/a is a noun which means
** _____.

151
Megal/o/cardi/a means enlargement or overdevelopment of the heart. When something causes overgrowth of the heart,
_____ / ____ / _____ / _____ results.

152
Megalocardia refers to heart muscle. When any muscle exercises, it gets larger. If the heart muscle has to overexercise,
_____ / ____ / _____ / _____
will probably occur.

153
Inadequate oxygen supply causes the heart muscle to beat more often. An inadequate amount of oxygen can lead to
_____.

154
Prolonged, severe asthma can cut down the supply of oxygen to the body. This kind of asthma, if not checked, will cause
_____.

155
Megal/o/gastr/ia means large or enlarged stomach. The word root for stomach is _____.

156
Megal/o means large. Gastr is the word root for stomach. **ia** is a noun ending. Form a noun that means large or enlargement of the stomach.
_____ / ____ / _____ / _____

157
When the stomach is so large it crowds other organs, an undesirable condition known as
_____ / ____ / _____ / _____ exists.

158
ia is a noun ending of condition. When megalogastria occurs, an undesirable _____
exists.

21

159

Mania is an English word that comes directly from the Greek word, mania, which means madness. Many mental disorders are compound words that end in this word, _____.

mania

160

Man/ia is a noun of condition. The condition is "madness" or, more properly, mental disorder. The ending that tells you mania is a noun and shows a condition is _____.

ia

161

Megal/o/man/ia is a symptom of a mental disorder in which the patient has delusions of grandeur. When a patient has a greatly enlarged opinion of himself, he suffers from

megal/o/man/ia
megalomania
meg a lo ma' ni a

_____/ /_____/_____.

162

People with megalomania are frequently found in mental hospitals. Many such hospitals have a patient who says he is King Solomon. One of this patient's symptoms is

megalomania

_____/ /_____/_____.

163

Many people think Adolf Hitler suffered from delusions of grandeur or

megalomania

_____.

164

Megal/o/cardi/a means ** _____

enlargement of
the heart

_____.

heart

Cardi is the word root for _____.

165

Cardi/o is used in building words that refer to the heart. Card/itis means ** _____

inflammation
of the heart

_____.

166

logy and **logist** are combining forms you will use as suffixes for convenience.

    logos   —Greek for study
    log/y   —noun, study of
    log/ist —noun, one who studies

A cardi/o/logist is a specialist in the study of diseases of the

heart

eases of the _____.

167

A/cardi/o/logist diagnoses heart disease. The specialist who determines that a heart is deformed is a

_____ / ___ / _____.

cardi/o/logist
cardiologist
kar di ol' o gist

168

A cardiologist discovers irregularities in the flow of the blood in the heart. The physician who catheterizes the heart is a

_____.

cardiologist

169

A man who reads electr/o/cardi/o/grams (records of electrical impulses given off by the heart) is also a

_____.

cardiologist

170

Give the meaning of electr/o/cardi/o/gram. (Gram/o is a combining form which means record.)
**

_____

_____ .

a record of electrical
waves given off by the
heart
(or equivalent)

171

Electrocardio/gram is the record. Electrocardio/graph is the instrument used to record the

___ / ___ _____ / ___ / ___ .

electr/o/cardi/o/gram
electrocardiogram
e lek tro kar' di o gram

172

The electr/o/cardi/o/gram is a record obtained by electr/o/cardi/o/graph/y. A technician can learn electrocardiography, but it takes a cardiologist to read the

___ / ___ _____ / ___ / ___ .

electrocardiogram

173

A physician can take a chart that looks like this, ⌇⌇⌇⌇⌇⌇⌇ , and learn something about a person's heart. He is a _____ _____ and is reading an

_____ .

cardiologist

electrocardiogram

174

algia is a suffix that means pain. Form a word that means heart pain. (Since algia is a suffix, you will use the word root rather than the combining form.)

_____ / _____ .

cardi/algia
cardialgia
kar di al' ji a

23

175

Gastr/algia means pain in the stomach. When a patient complains of pain in the heart, his symptom is known medically as

cardialgia

_____.

176

algia

The suffix for pain is _____.

177

You used the word megal/o/gastr/ia for enlarged stomach. Gastr/o is the combining form for

stomach

_____.

178

Gastr/ectomy means excision (removal) of all or part of the stomach. Ectomy is a combining form that you may use as a suffix. Ectomy means

excision or removal

_____.

179

This is a free frame for those who are interested. Others may go on.

ect/o	combining form–outside
t om/e	cut
y	noun ending
ect om y	excision

180

gastr/ectomy
gastrectomy
gas trek' to mi

A gastr/ectomy is a surgical procedure. When a stomach ulcer has perforated, a partial

_____/_____ may be indicated.

181

gastrectomy

Cancer of the stomach will result in a

_____.

182

gastr/itis
gastritis
gas tri' tis

Form a word that means inflammation of the stomach. _____/_____.

183

Duoden/o is used in words that refer to the first part of the small intestine, the duoden/um. To build words about the duodenum, use

duoden/o

_____/_____.

24

184

The duoden/um is the part of the small intestine that connects with the stomach. Duoden/o is a word root–combining form that refers to the

duodenum
du o dē' num

_____/_____.

185

Gastr/o/duoden/ostomy means formation of a new opening between the stomach and duodenum. **ostomy** is a combining form you can use as a suffix to mean **forming an opening.** Gastr/o/duoden/ostomy means ** _____

forming an opening
between the stomach
and duodenum

_____.

186

Here's another free frame for those interested in ostomy.

ost/i	mouth—opening
tom/e	cut
y	noun ending
make a **mouth**	(opening) by cutting

187

Gastr/o/duoden/ostomy means forming an opening between the stomach and duodenum. A surgeon who removes the natural connection between the duodenum and stomach, and then forms a new connection, is doing a

gastr/o/duoden/ostomy
gastroduodenostomy
gas tro du o den os' to mi

_____/____/_____/_____.

188

A gastroduodenostomy is a surgical procedure. When the pyloric sphincter, a valve that controls the amount of food going from the stomach to the duodenum, no longer functions, a _____

gastroduodenostomy

_____ may be done.

189

When a portion of the first part of the small intestine is removed because of cancer, a new opening is formed by performing a

gastroduodenostomy
or
duodenostomy

_____.

190

o/tom/y is a combining form you may use as a suffix because it connects directly to a word root. A duo/den/otomy is an incision into the

duodenum

_____.

25

191

otomy

If a duo/den/otomy is an incision into the duodenum, the suffix for **incision** is _____.

192

duoden/otomy
duodenotomy
du o den ot' o me

otomy means incision into. An incision into the duodenum is a

_____.

193

duoden/otomy

If a growth has to be removed from the inner wall of the duodenum, a _____ _____ is done.

194

duodenotomy

Any time a surgeon incises the duodenum, he is performing a _____.

195

itis
duoden/itis
duodenitis
du o den i' tis

The suffix for inflammation is _____. The word for inflammation of the duodenum is

_____.

196

duodenitis

itis indicates a general symptomatic term. When a physician is listing symptoms about the duodenum and he wants to say it is inflamed, he uses the word _____.

197

al

Duoden/al is an adjective. **al** is an adjectival ending meaning pertaining to (whatever the adjective modifies). One adjectival ending is _____.

198

duoden/al   duodenal
du o de' nal
ulcer
lesion

In **duoden/al ulcer** and **duoden/al lesion,** the adjective is _____ / _____ and the nouns modified are _____ and

_____.

199

duodenal

In the sentence, "Duodenal carcinoma was present," the adjective meaning pertaining to the duodenum is _____.

200

duodenal

The adjectival form of duoden/o is

_____ / _____.

201

The suffix ostomy means making a new opening. The word to form a new opening into the duodenum is

duoden/ostomy
duodenostomy
du o den os' to me

_____/_____.

202

A duodenostomy **can** be formed in more than one manner. If it is formed with the stomach, it is called a

gastroduodenostomy

_____/___/_____/_____.

203

The suffix for forming a new opening is

ostomy

_____.

Use the material in the following chart to work the next 14 frames.

WORDS ARE FORMED BY

I. Word root + suffix
  a. dermat/itis
  b. cyan/osis
  c. duoden/al
II. Combining form + word root + suffix
    (this can be a word itself)
  a. acr/o/cyan/osis
  b. leuk/o/cyte
  c. megal/o/man/ia
III. Any number of combining forms + word root + suffix
  a. leuk/o/cyt/o/pen/ia
  b. electr/o/cardi/o/graph/y

204

word root

suffix

In I(a) dermat is the *_____.

        itis   is the _____.

205

word root

suffix

In I(b) cyan is the *_____.

        osis is the _____.

206

duoden

al

In I(c) the word root is _____.

    the suffix is   _____.

27

207

combining form   In II(a)   acr/o   is the *_____.

word root   cyan   is the *_____.

suffix   osis   is the _____.

208

combining form   In II(b)   leuk/o   is the *_____.

word root   cyt   is the *_____.

suffix   e   is the _____.

209

combining form   In III(a)   leuk/o   is a *_____.

combining form   cyt/o   is a *_____.

word root   pen   is a *_____.

suffix   ia   is a _____.

210

In III(b) the first combining form is

electr/o

_____ / ___.

the second combining form is

cardi/o

_____ / ___.

graph   the word root is _____.

y   the suffix that makes it a noun is ___.

211

Form a word without even knowing its meaning in the next four frames. Use what is needed from encephal/o + itis:

encephal/itis

_____ / _____.

212

Use what is needed from   encephal/o

                            malac/o

                            ia

encephal/o/malac/ia

_____ / _ / _____ / ___.

213

Use what is needed from   encephal/o

                            mening/o

                            itis

encephal/o/mening/
itis

_____ / _ / _____ / ___.

214

Use what is needed from   encephal/o

                            myel/o

                            path/o

encephal/o/myel/o/
path/y

                            y

_____ / _ / _____ / _ / _____.

215

A prefix goes before a word to change its meaning. In the words hyper/trophy, hyper/emia, and hyper/emesis, hyper changes the meaning of trophy, emia, and emesis. **hyper** is a _____.

prefix

216

hyper is a prefix that means above or more than normal. To say that a person was overly critical, you would use the word

_____ / critic / al .

hyper

217

Hyper/thyroid/ism means overactivity of the thyroid gland. The prefix that means the thyroid gland is secreting more than normal is _____.

hyper

218

Emesis is a word that means vomiting. A word that means excessive vomiting is

_____ / _____ .

hyper/emesis
hyperemesis
hi per em' e sis

219

Hyperemesis gravidarum is a complication of pregnancy that can require hospitalization. The part of the disorder that tells you excessive vomiting occurs is _____.

hyperemesis

220

Gallbladder attacks can cause excessive vomiting. This, too, is called

_____ .

hyperemesis

221

Hyper/trophy means overdevelopment. Troph/o comes from the Greek word for nourishment. See the connection between nourishment and development. Overdevelopment is called

_____ / _____ .

hyper/trophy
hypertrophy
hi per' tro fi

222

Many organs can hypertrophy. If the heart overdevelops, the condition is _____ of the heart.

hypertrophy

223

Muscles also can overdevelop or

_____ .

hypertrophy

224

hypo is a prefix that is just the opposite of **hyper.** The prefix for under or less than normal is

hypo

_____.

225

Hypo/trophy means progressive degeneration. When an organ or tissue that has developed properly wastes away or decreases in size, it is undergoing _____/_____ .

hypo/trophy
hypotrophy
hi pot' ro fi

226

Hypotrophy occurs in many tissues. When muscles are not exercised or used, they undergo

hypotrophy

_____.

227

Derm/o refers to _____. Derm/ic makes the word an adjective. Hypo/derm/ic is an adjective that means under the _____.

skin

skin

228

In hypo/derm/ic, **ic** as a suffix forms an _____ _____ (adjective/noun). A needle that is inserted under the skin is a _____ needle.

adjective
hypo/derm/ic
hypodermic
hi po der' mic

229

A hypodermic needle is short because it goes just under the skin. A shot that can be given superficially is administered with a _____ needle.

hypodermic

230

In hypodermic, the prefix is _____ and means _____; the suffix is _____ and forms an _____ (part of speech).

hypo
under
ic
adjective

231

Aden/o is used in words that refer to glands. The word root is _____. The combining form is _____/_____ .

aden

aden/o

232

Build a word that means inflammation of a gland (word root + suffix rule)

aden/itis
adenitis
ad en i' tis

_____/_____ .

233

Aden/ectomy means excision or removal of a gland.
The part that means excision is

_____.

The part that means gland is _____.
The word for removal of a gland is

_____/_____.

ectomy
aden
aden/ectomy
adenectomy
ad en ek' to mi

234

An adenectomy is a surgical procedure. If a gland
is tumorous, part or all of it may be excised. This
operation is an _____.

adenectomy

235

oma is the suffix for tumor (word root + suffix
rule). Form a word that means tumor of a gland.

_____/_____.

aden/oma
adenoma
ad en o' ma

236

Sometimes the thyroid gland develops an adenoma.
In this case, a patient's history might read, ". . .
hyperthyroidism noted—due to presence of a thyroid _____."

adenoma

237

When a thyroid _____ (tumor of
a gland) is found, a partial _____
(excision of gland) is performed.

adenoma
adenectomy or
(thyroidectomy)

238

Path/o is the combining form for disease. Aden/
o/path/y means any disease of a gland. In this
word you have a combining form + a *_____
_____ + a suffix to form the word

_____/_____/_____/_____.

word root
aden/o/path/y
adenopathy
ad en op' a thi

239

Adenopathy means glandular disease in general.
When the diagnosis is made of a diseased gland,
but the disease is not specifically known or stated,
the word used is _____.

adenopathy

240

An _____ (glandular
disease) could be diagnosed as an _____
(glandular tumor). If so, the surgeon may want to
have an _____ (excision of a
gland) performed.

adenopathy
adenoma

adenectomy

i has a y sound

241

When a gland is found to have a mild

adenitis

_____/_____ (inflammation), no

adenectomy

_____/_____ (surgery) is indicated.

242

An adenoma is a glandular tumor. **oma** is the suf-

tumor

fix for _____. A lip/oma is a tumor
containing fat. Lip/o is the word root–combining

fat

form for _____.

243

lip/oma
lipoma
li po' ma

A lip/oma is seldom malignant (cancerous). A fatty

tumor is called a _____/_____.

244

lipoma
lipoma
lipoma
lipoma

Write lipoma four times:

    fatty tumor _____/_____ _____

    fatty tumor _____ _____

Work Review Sheets 1 and 2.

245

cancerous tumor or
malignant tumor

Carcin/o is the word root–combining form for
cancer. A carcin/oma is a
    **

_____.

246

A carcinoma may occur in almost any part of the
body. A stomach cancer is called gastric

carcinoma

_____/_____.

247

The bloodstream may carry a carcinoma to other
parts of the body. The intestine has a rich blood

carcinoma

supply. For this reason, intestinal _____
is extremely dangerous.

248

Cancer of the spleen is called splenic

carcinoma

_____.

Cancer of the tonsil is tonsillar

carcinoma

_____.

Cancer of the duodenum is duodenal

carcinoma

_____.

249

The combining form for fat is _____/_____.

oid is a suffix which means like or resembling. Build a word which means fatlike or resembling fat.

_____/_____.

lip/o
lip/oid

lip/oid
lip' oid

250

The word lipoid is used in chemistry or pathology. It describes a substance that looks like fat, dissolves like fat, but is not _____. A word that means resembling fat is _____.

fat

lipoid

251

In proper amounts, cholesterol is essential to health, but too much may cause arteriosclerosis. Cholesterol is an alcohol that resembles fat; therefore, it is a

_____.

lipoid

252

Muc/oid means resembling mucus. **oid** is a suffix meaning _____. The word root for mucus is _____, and its combining form is _____/_____.

resembling

muc

muc/o

253

Mucoid is an adjective that means resembling or like mucus. There is a substance in connective tissue that resembles mucus. This is a

_____/_____ substance.

muc/oid
mucoid
mu' koyd

254

There is a protein in the body that resembles mucus. This protein is said to be _____ in nature.

mucoid

255

Anything that resembles mucus is called a

_____.

mucoid

256

Muc/us is a secretion of the muc/ous membrane. **us** is a noun suffix. **ous** is an adjectival suffix. The muc/ous membrane secretes _____/_____.

muc/us
mucus
mu' kus

257

Mucus is secreted by cells in the nose. It traps dust and bacteria from the air. One of the body's protective devices is _____.

mucus

258

The mucous membrane secretes _____.
The tissue that secretes mucus is the

_____ / _____ membrane or muc/osa.

mucus
muc/ous
mucous
mu' kus

259

The noun (the secretion) built from muc/o is
_____. The adjective (pertaining to) built
from muc/o is _____.

mucus
mucous

260

The mucous membrane or mucosa is found lining
the body openings. This protective, mucous membrane can also be called the _____ / _____.

muc/osa

261

The mucosa secretes _____. Anything
that resembles mucus is _____.
Mucoid substances are not mucus; therefore, they
are not secreted by the
** _____.

mucus
mucoid

mucosa or
mucous membrane

262

Laryng/o is used to build words that refer to the
larynx. The larynx contains the vocal cords. When
referring to the organ of sound, use

_____ / _____.

laryng/o

263

The word root for laryng/o is _____.
The word root is used when adding a

_____.

laryng

suffix

264

Form a word that means inflammation of the larynx.
_____ / _____.

laryng/itis
laryngitis
lar in **ji'** tis

265

Laryng/algia means laryngeal (pronounce **lar in'
je al**) pain. Laryng is the word root. The suffix for
pain is _____.

algia

266

After a bad cold, a patient may have laryng/itis
with accompanying pain. Pain in the larynx is
called _____ / _____.

laryng/algia
laryngalgia
lar in **gal'** ji a

34

267

Cancer of the larynx may cause pain or

laryngalgia _____ .

268

An inflammation of the nerves of the larynx can

laryngalgia also cause _____ .

269

Laryng/ostomy means making a new opening into the larynx. When a new source of air is needed for breathing or speaking, a

laryng/ostomy
laryngostomy
lar in **gos'** to mi   _____ / _____ is done.

270

Anything that obstructs the flow of air from the nose to the larynx may call for a

laryngostomy   _____ / _____ .

271

ostomy means creating a new opening that will be permanent. When a permanent opening has been made through the neck and into the larynx, a

laryngostomy _____ has been performed.

272

The word ending for new opening is

ostomy _____ .

273

When a **temporary opening** is wanted into the larynx, the surgical procedure is a laryng/**otomy.** An incision into the larynx is called a

laryng/otomy
laryngotomy
lar in got' o mi   _____ / _____ .

274

When a patient has pneumonia and a freer flow of air is desired, the surgeon may incise the larynx

laryngotomy (or
laryngostomy) and thus do a _____ .

275

The word that means making an incision into the

laryngotomy larynx is _____ .

276

At this stage of word building, students sometimes find that they have one big pain in the head. The word for pain in the head is cephal/algia. The word

cephal root for head is _____ .

35

277

If you are suffering from cephalalgia, persevere, for later this gets to be fun. Any pain in the head may be called

_____ / _____ .

cephal/algia
cephalalgia
sef a lal' ji a

278

The word root–combining form for head is cephal/o. The word for pain in the head is

_____ .

cephalalgia

279

Another word for pain in the head is cephal/o/dyn/ia. This word shows the combining form before the word root + a suffix. If this seems a headache, relax. Either word,

_____ / _____ / _____ / _____

or _____ / _____ will do for headache.

cephal/o/dyn/ia
cephalodynia
sef al o din' i a

cephalalgia

280

algia and **dyn/ia** are usually interchangeable. The combining form requires _____ / _____ , while a word root takes the suffix

_____ .

dyn/ia

algia

281

Dynia can take the adjectival form dyn/ic. An adjective that means pertaining to head pain is

_____ / _____ / _____ .

cephal/o/dyn/ic
cephalodynic
sef al o din' ic

282

To say medically that headache discomfort exists, use the adjective

_____ / _____ / _____ .

for headache.

cephal/o/dyn/ic

283

Two nouns for head pain are

_____ / _____ and

_____ / _____ / _____ .

The adjective used for head pain is

_____ / _____ / _____ .

cephalalgia

cephalodynia

cephalodynic

284

Cephal/ic means pertaining to or toward the head. Cephal/ic is an _____ (noun/adjective). This is evident because cephalic ends in _____.

adjective

ic

285

Cephalic is an adjective. A case history reporting head cuts due to an accident might read,

"_____ / _____ lacerations present."

cephal/ic
cephalic
sef al' ic

286

In the phrase, "lack of cephalic orientation," the adjective is _____.

cephalic

287

Another phrase might be, "_____ tumors noted."

cephalic

288

Inside the head, **en**closed in bone, is the brain. **En**cephal/o is used in words pertaining to the brain. Build a word meaning inflammation of the brain.

_____ / _____.

encephal/itis
encephalitis
en sef a li' tis

289

The suffix for tumor is _____. Use what is necessary from encephal/o to build a word for brain tumor. _____ / _____.

oma
encephal/oma

encephaloma
en sef al o' ma

290

The Greek word for hernia is kēle. From this, you derive the combining form cele/o or o/cele. Encephal/o/cele is a word meaning herniation of _____ tissue.

brain

291

An encephalocele occurs when some brain tissue protrudes through a cranial fissure. The word for herniation of brain tissue is

_____ / _____ / _____.

encephal/o/cele
encephalocele
en sef' al o sēl

292

Any hernia is a projection of a part from its natural cavity. Herniation is indicated by **cele**. A projection of brain tissue from its natural cavity is an

_____ / _____ / _____.

encephal/o/cele

293

Brain herniation is sometimes a symptom of hydro-cephaly. This symptom, in medical language, is called an

encephalocele

_____ / ___ / _____ .

294

The noun for protrusion of brain tissue through a cranial fissure is

encephalocele

_____ .

295

Malac/ia is a word meaning softening of a tissue. Encephal/o/malac/ia means ** _____

softening of brain tissue

_____ .

296

Malac/o is the combining form. The word root is

malac _s h_

_____ .

297

Encephal/o/malac/ia ends in **ia. ia** is a suffix that forms a noun. A noun meaning softening of brain tissue is

encephal/o/malac/ia
encephalomalacia
en sef al o mal a' si a

_____ / ___ / _____ / _____ .

298

An accident causing brain injury could result in the softening of some brain tissue, or

encephalomalacia

_____ .

299

Some brain diseases can also cause softening and produce the symptom,

encephalomalacia

_____ .

300

Using what is necessary from malac/o with the suffix otomy, form a word which means incision of soft areas:

malac/otomy _k_
malacotomy
mal a kot' o mi

_____ / _____ .

301

Osteopathy means disease of the bones. From this form the word root–combining form for bone.

oste/o

_____ / _____ .

38

oste/itis
osteitis
os te i' tis

302
A word meaning inflammation of bones is

_____/_____.

oste/o/malac/ia
osteomalacia
os te o mal a' si a

303
Oste/o/malac/ia means softening of the bones. To say that bones have lost a detectable amount of their hardness, use the noun

_____/____/_____/_____.

oste/o/malac/ia

304
One cause of oste/o/malac/ia is the removal of calcium from the bones. When calcium is removed from the bones and they lose some of their hardness, a disorder

_____/____/_____/_____,

results.

osteomalacia

305
A disorder of the parathyroid gland can cause calcium to be withdrawn from the bones. When this occurs,

_____/____/_____/_____,

results.

osteomalacia

306
When there is not enough calcium in the diet, this same disorder, _____, can occur.

oste/o/path/y

307
Form a word that means disease of bone:

_____/____/_____/_____.

osteoma

308
A hard outgrowth on a bone may be a bone tumor or _____/_____.

joint

309
Path/o means disease. Oste/o/arthr/o/path/y is a noun that means any disease involving bones and joints. Arthr/o is used in words to mean

_____.

310

Oste/o/arthr/o/path/y is a compound noun. Analyze it:

oste/o

arthr/o
path
y
oste/o/arthr/o/path/y
osteoarthropathy
os te o ar throp' a thi

_____ /_____ bone (combining form)

_____ /_____ joint (combining form)

_____ disease (word root)

_____ noun (suffix)

Now put it together:

_____ / / _____ / / _____ / .

311

Osteoarthropathy is often associated with other diseases. When there is bone and joint involvement along with lung disease, it could be

osteoarthropathy

_____ .

312

Arthr/o/plast/y means surgical repair of a joint. Plast/y means

surgical repair

* _____ .

313

Think of a plast/ic surgeon building a new nose or doing a face lifting. These are surgical repairs. Plast/o means

surgical repair

* _____ .

314

surgical repair of a joint

Arthr/o/plast/y means ** _____

_____ .

315

Arthr/o/plast/y may take many forms. When a joint has lost its ability to move, movement can sometimes be restored by an

arthr/o/plast/y

_____ / / _____ / .

316

Arthroplasty is a noun. If a child is born without a joint, sometimes one can be formed for him by a surgical procedure called

arthroplasty

_____ .

317

The physician calls surgical repair of a joint an

arthroplasty

_____ .

40

arthr/itis
arthritis
ar thri' tis

318
Form a word that means inflammation of a joint:
_____/_____.

arthr/otomy
arthrotomy
arth rot' o mi

319
You're getting to be pretty good at this, aren't you?
Form a word that means incision of a joint:
_____/_____.

320
The word oste/o/chondr/itis means inflammation
of bone and cartilage. The word root–combining

chondr/o

form for cartilage is _____/ o .

321
Cartilage is a tough, elastic connective tissue found
in the ear, nose tip, and rib ends. The lining of

cartilage

joints also contains _____.

322
Analyze oste/o/chondr/itis:

oste/o
chondr
itis
oste/o/chondr/itis
osteochondritis
os te o kon dri' tis

_____/ combining form for bone
_____ word root for cartilage
_____ suffix for inflammation
Now put the parts together:
_____/_____/_____/_____.

323
Form a word meaning pain in or around cartilage:
_____/_____

chondr/algia
chondr/o/dyn/ia

(word root + suffix) or
_____/_____/_____/_____.

You pronounce.

(combining form for cartilage).

324
Chondr/ectomy means

excision of cartilage

** _____.

325
Chondr/o/cost/al means pertaining to rib cartilage.

ribs

Cost/o is used in words about the _____.

326
Form a word that means excision of a rib or ribs:

cost/ectomy
costectomy
kos tek' to mi

_____/_____.

327

Chondr/o/cost/al is an adjective. This is evident because **al** is the ending for an

adjective _____.

328

Chondrocost/al means pertaining to the ribs and cartilage. **al** forms an adjective that means

pertaining to _____.
        *

329

Analyze chondr/o/cost/al:

chondr/o   _____ /   cartilage.

cost   _____   rib.

al   _____   suffix.

chondr/o/cost/al   Now put them together:
kon dro kos' tal

pertaining to ribs   _____ / ___ / _____ .
and cartilage

This means * _____

_____ .

330

cost/al   Form a word that means pertaining to the ribs:
costal
kos' tal   _____ / _____ .

331

Inter/cost/al means between the ribs. The prefix

inter   for between is _____ .

332

Form a word that means between cartilages

inter/chondr/al   _____ / _____ .
interchondral
in ter kon' dral   (adjective)

333

Inter/cost/al means between the ribs. **inter** is the

between   prefix that means _____ .

334

Inter/cost/al may refer to the muscles between the ribs. These muscles that move the ribs when breath-

inter/cost/al   ing are the
intercostal
in ter kos' tal   _____ / _____ muscles.

335

One set of intercostal muscles enlarges the rib cage when breathing in. When exhaling, the rib cage is

intercostal   made smaller by another set of _____
muscles.

42

336

Inter/dent/al means between the teeth. The word root for tooth is _____.

dent

337

An inter/dent/al cavity occurs

between the teeth

$$** \underline{\hspace{10cm}}.$$

338

Inter/dent/al is an adjective so it must modify a noun. In "interdental spaces" the adjective is

inter/dent/al
interdental
in ter den' tal

_____ / _____ / _____.

339

In "interdental cavity" the adjective is

interdental

_____.

340

Form an adjective that means pertaining to the teeth. _____ / _____.

dent/al
dental
den' tal

341

Pain in the teeth, or a toothache, is called

dent/algia
dentalgia
den tal' ji a

_____ / _____.

342

oid is the suffix that means like or resembling. Form a word that means tooth shaped or resembling a tooth: _____ / _____.

dent/oid
dentoid
den' toid

343

A dent/ist takes care of _____.

teeth

A dent/ifrice is used for cleaning _____.

teeth

344

Ab/norm/al is a word that means deviating (turning away) from what is normal. **ab** is a

pre/fix

_____ / fix that means **from.**

345

Ab/normal is used in ordinary English. If abnormal is in your usable vocabulary, skip this frame. If you have **never** used the word abnormal, write it five times.

ab/normal
abnormal
ab nor' mal

_____   _____

_____   _____

_____

43

346

ab is a prefix that means from or away from. Abnormal means *_____
normal.

away from

347

ab is a prefix that means

*_____.

from or away from

348

Ab/errant uses the prefix ab before the English
word for wandering. Ab/errant means **_____

_____.

wandering from (the
normal course of events)

349

Ab/errant is used in medicine to describe a struc-
ture that wanders from the normal. When some
nerve fibers follow an unusual route, they form an

_____/_____ nerve.

ab/errant
aberrant
ab er' ant

350

Aberrant nerves wander from the normal nerve
track. Blood vessels that follow a path of their own
are _____ vessels.

aberrant

351   *f sound*

In the body, lymphatics often follow an _____
course.

aberrant

352

Ab/duct/ion means movement away from a mid-
line. When the hand is raised from the side of the

body, _____/_____/_____ has occurred.

ab/duct/ion
abduction
ab duc' shun

353

Abduction can occur from any midline. When the
fingers of the hand are spread apart, _____
has occurred in four fingers.

abduction

354

When a child has been kidnapped and taken from
his parents, he has been _____
(past tense verb).

abducted

355

ad is a prefix meaning toward. Movement toward a

midline is _____/_____.

ad/duction
adduction
ad duc' shun

356

Addiction means being drawn toward some habit. The person who takes drugs habitually suffers from

drug _____/_____.

ad/diction
addiction
a dik' shun

357

Addiction implies habit. Alcoholism is

_____/_____ to alcohol.

addiction

358

A person addicted to drugs is a drug addict. A person addicted to gambling is a gambling

_____.

addict

359

An ad/hesion is formed when two normally separate tissues join together. They adhere to each other. Adhering to another part forms an

_____/_____.

ad/hesion
adhesion
ad he' shun

360

Several years ago, adhesions occurred frequently following surgery. Patients did not walk soon enough so tissues healed together. Following an

appendectomy, _____/_____
were common.

adhesions

361

Now patients walk the day following an appendectomy. This has practically eliminated

_____.

adhesions

362

Patients walk within a day after most abdominal surgery. This has nearly eliminated

_____.

adhesions

Rework Review Sheets 1 and 2. Just cover your answers with a folded piece of paper.

363 change combining faⁱⁿ

Abdomin/o is used to form words about the abdomen. When you see abdomin/o any place in a word, you think about the _____.

abdomen
ab do' men

364

Abdomin/al is an adjective that means ** _____

_____.

pertaining to the
abdomen

45

365

Abdomin/o/centesis means tapping or puncture of the abdomen. This is a surgical puncture. The word for surgical puncture of the abdomen is

/ /
_____.

abdomin/o/centesis
abdominocentesis
ab dom i no sen te' sis

366

Centesis (surgical puncture) is a word in itself. Build a word meaning surgical puncture, puncture, or tapping of the abdomen:

_____.

abdominocentesis

367

When fluid has accumulated in the abdomin/al cavity, it can be drained off by an

_____.

abdominocentesis

368

The word for surgical puncture of the heart is

/ /
_____.

cardi/o/centesis
cardiocentesis
kar di o sen te' sis

369

Abdomin/o/cyst/ic means pertaining to the abdomen and bladder. Analyze the word:

/
_____ combining form
_____ word root
_____ suffix

Now put them together to form the word:

/ / /
_____.

abdomin/o
cyst
ic
abdomin/o/cyst/ic
abdominocystic
ab dom i no sis' tik

370

From abdomin/o/cyst/ic you see that the word root for bladder is _____.

cyst

371

Cyst/o is used to form words that refer to the

_____.

bladder

372

To refer to the urinary bladder, or **any sac containing fluid,** use some form of _____ /____.

cyst/o

373

The word for incision into the bladder is

/
_____.

cyst/otomy
cystotomy
sist ot' o mi

46

cyst/ectomy cystectomy sis tek' to mi	**374** The word for excision of the bladder is _____ / _____ .
cyst/o/cele cystocele sis' to sel	**375** A herniation of the bladder is a _____ / ___ / cele .
cystocele	**376** When the bladder herniates into the vagina, a _____ is formed.

377
Abdomin/o/thorac/ic means pertaining to the abdomen and thorax. The thorax is the chest. Analyze this word:

abdomin/o	_____ / abdomen
thorac	_____ thorax
ic	_____ adjective—pertaining to

abdomin/o/thorac/ic abdominothoracic ab dom i no tho ras' ik	Now put them together to form _____ / __ / _____ / _____ .

abdominothoracic	**378** Abdomin/o/thorac/ic pain means, literally, pertaining to pain in the abdomen and chest. If a physician wanted to say that there were lesions in these areas he could say _____ / __ / _____ / _____ lesions.
thorac/ic thoracic thor as' ik	**379** Thorac/o is used to form words about the thorax or chest. A word that means pertaining to the chest is _____ / _____ .
thorac/otomy thoracotomy tho rak ot' o mi	**380** A word that means incision of the chest is _____ / _____ .
thorac/o/centesis thoracocentesis tho rak o sen te' sis	**381** A word that means surgical tapping of the chest to remove fluids is _____ / __ / _____ . (surgical puncture)

thorac/o/path/y
thoracopathy
tho rak op' ath i

382
A word that means any chest disease is
_____ / / _____ / ____.

thorac/o/plast/y
thoracoplasty
tho' ra ko plas ti

383
A word for surgical repair of the chest is
_____ / / plast / y ____.

cyst/o/plast/y
cystoplasty
sis' to plas ti

384
A word for surgical repair of the bladder is
_____ / / _____ / ____.

water or fluid
or
watery fluid

385
A hydr/o/cyst is a sac (or bladder) filled with watery fluid. Hydr/o is used in words to mean
_____.

hydr/o/cephal/us
hydrocephalus
hi dro sef' a lus

386
Hydr/o/cephal/us is characterized by an enlarged head due to increased amount of fluid in the skull. A collection of fluid in the head is called
_____ / / _____ / ____.

Hydrocephalus

387
Hydrocephalus, unless arrested, results in deformity. The face seems small. The eyes are abnormal. The head is large. _____
_____ also causes brain damage.

hydrocephalus

388
Because of the damage to the brain, children with
_____ are
usually mentally retarded.

Hydr/o/cephal/ic
hydrocephalic
hi dro se fal' ic

389
Hydrocephalus is the noun. The adjectival ending is ic. _____ / / _____ / _____
children can be seen in homes for the mentally retarded.

abnormal fear

390
Hydr/o/phob/ia means having an abnormal fear of water. Phob/ia means
**_____.

abnormal fear

391
Phob/ia is a word meaning any
**_____.

392

In your medical dictionary find the word phobia. How many phobias do you recognize already? ** _____ . An abnormal fear of

between 3 and 12
hydr/o/phob/ia
hydrophobia

hi dro fo' bi a

water is _____ / / ____ / ____ .

393

Some parents are abnormally afraid to have their children swim or even ride in a boat. These parents suffer from

hydro/phobia

_____ / _____ .

394

There is also a disease acquired from the bite of a rabid dog called

hydrophobia

_____ .

395

hydr/o/therap/y
hydrotherapy
hi dro ther' a pi

Therap/y means treatment. Treatment by water is _____ / / _____ / ____ .

396

Swirling water baths are a form of

hydrotherapy

_____ .

397

Lumb/o builds words about the loin. Lumb/ar is the adjectiv/al form. An **adjective** meaning pertain-

lumb/ar
lŭm' bar

ing to the loin is _____ / _____ .

398

There are five lumb/ar vertebrae. Low back (loin)

lumbar

pain is called _____ / _____ pain.

399

lumbar

There is also a reflex called the _____ reflex.

400

adjective
pertaining to the chest
and loin or something
near this

Thorac/o/lumb/ar is a _____ (noun/adjective) meaning ** _____ _____ .

401

supra

Supra/lumb/ar means above the lumbar region. A prefix which means above is _____ .

402

above the lumbar region
or above the loin

Supra/lumb/ar means ** _____ _____ .

49

403

Supra/cost/al means

above the ribs

_____.

404

Supra/pub/ic means above the pubic. Pub/o is used in words about the _____.

pubis
pu' bis

405

The suprapubic region is above the arch of the pub/is. When the bladder is incised above the pubis, an incision is made in the

supra/pub/ic
suprapubic
su pra pu' bik

_____/_____/_____ region.

406

"The incision is made in the suprapubic region." From this sentence pick out:

the adjective: _____

suprapubic

two nouns: _____

incision

_____

region

407

There is also a reflex called the _____
reflex.

suprapubic

408

Try to figure out what surgery is done in a **supra/
pubic cyst/otomy** **_____

anything close to
incision of bladder from
the suprapubic region

_____.

409

The pub/is is a bone of the pelvis. Pub/is is a

noun

_____ (noun/adjective).

410

From pub/o form a noun: _____.

pubis

an adjective: _____.

pubic

411

The pub/ic bone is also called the _____/_____.

pubis

412

The pelv/is is formed by the pelv/ic bones. Pelv/i

pelv/is
pelvis
pel' vis

refers to the _____/_____ (noun).

413

Pelv/i/metr/y is done during pregnancy to find the measurements of the pelvis. To find a woman's pelvic size, the physician does

pelv/i/metr/y
pelvimetry
pel vim' et ri

_____/____/_____/_____.

414

Look up pelvimetry or pelvis in your dictionary. (Keep the dictionary open for frame 416.) See the pictures showing how pelvimetry is done. Taking pelvic measurements is called

pelvimetry

_____ .

415

A physician can determine whether or not a woman may have trouble during labor by doing

pelvimetry

_____ .

416

Look in the dictionary for a word that names the device used for pelvimetry. It is a

pelv/i/meter
pelvimeter
pel vim' et er

_____ .

417

The pelvimeter measures different diameters. Pelvimetry is done by reading a scale of numbers on

pelvimeter

the _____ / _____ / _____ .

418

pelvimeter

To measure the pelvis, the _____
is used.

419

A meter is an instrument to measure.

instrument

A speed/o/meter is an _____
to measure speed.

instrument

A pelv/i/meter is an _____
to measure the pelvis.

420

measures

A cyt/o/meter _____ cells.

measures

A cephal/o/meter _____ the skull.

thorac/o/meter
tho ra kom' et er

A _____ / _____ / _____

measures the chest.

cardi/o/meter
kar di om' e ter

A _____ / _____ / _____

measures the heart.

421

supra/pelv/ic
suprapelvic
su pra pel' vic

The adjective meaning **above** the pelvis is

_____ / _____ / _____ .

51

422

above

Supra/crani/al refers to the surface of the head
_____ the skull.

423

surgical repair of
the skull or cranium

Crani/o is used in words referring to the crani/um
or skull. Crani/o/plast/y means ** _____
_____ .

424

crani/o/malac/ia
craniomalacia
kra ni o mal a' si a

The word for softening of the bones of the skull is
crani / o / _____ / _____ .

425

crani/ectomy
craniectomy
kra ni ek' to mi

The word meaning **excision** of part of the cranium
is _____ / _____ .

426

crani/otomy
craniotomy
kra ni ot' o mi

The word for **incision** into the skull is
_____ / _____ .

427

crani/o/meter
craniometer
kra ni om' et er

An instrument to measure the cranium is the
_____ / ____ / _____ .

428

cranial

cranial

There are cranial bones. There are also _____
nerves. There are even _____ fissures.

429

adjective

Crani/al is the _____ (noun/
adjectival) form of crani/o.

430

cerebr/um
cerebrum
ser' e brum

Crani/o/cerebr/al refers to the skull and the
cerebr/um. The cerebr/um is a part of the brain.
Cerebr/o is used to build words about the
_____ / _____ .

431

cerebrum

The cerebrum is the part of the brain in which
thought occurs. Man can think. Generally speaking, animals cannot. Man has a better-developed
_____ than animals.

432

cerebrum

Feeling is interpreted in the cerebrum. Motor impulses also arise in the _____.

433

cerebrum

Thinking, feeling, and movement are controlled by the gray matter of the _____.
(Were you ever told to use your "gray matter"? This is why.)

434

cerebr/al
cerebral
ser' e bral

The adjectival form of cerebrum is

_____ / _____.

Work Review Sheet 5.

435

cerebral

There is a cerebral reflex. There are cerebral fissures. You have probably heard of _____ hemorrhage.

436

inflammation of
the cerebrum

Cerebr/itis means ** _____

_____.

437

cerebral tumor or
any mass in the brain

A cerebr/oma is a
** _____.

438

any disease of the
cerebrum or disease
of the cerebrum

Cerebr/o/path/y means ** _____

_____.

439

cerebr/otomy
cerebrotomy
ser e brot' o mi

An incision into the cerebrum to remove an abscess

is a _____ / _____.

440

cerebr/o/spin/al
cerebrospinal
ser e bro spi' nal

Cerebr/o/spin/al refers to the brain and spinal cord. There is fluid that bathes the cerebrum and spinal cord. It is

_____ / _____ / _____ / _____.

fluid.

441

cerebrospinal

A cerebr/o/spin/al puncture is sometimes done to remove _____ fluid.

53

442

cerebrospinal

There is even a disease called _____ meningitis.

443

Mening/itis means inflammation of the meninges. The meninges are three membranes that cover the brain and spinal cord. The protective coverings of the brain and cord are

mening/es
meninges
min in' jez

_____ / _____ .

444

A meningocele is a herniation of the

meninges

_____ .

445

Mening/o/malac/ia means softening of the

meninges

_____ .

446

Mening/itis can occur as cerebr/al meningitis, as spin/al mening/itis, or as cerebr/o/spin/al

mening/itis
meningitis
men in ji' tis

_____ / _____ .

447

Look up meningitis in your dictionary. Read about the disease. Fill in the following blank. There are _____ (a number) kinds of meningitis listed.

14 to 37 depending on
the dictionary used.

448

There are many kinds of meningitis. The tubercle bacillus can cause tuberculous meningitis. Mening/o/cocc/i are bacteria that cause epidemic

meningitis

_____ .

449

Cocc/i is the plural of cocc/us. When building words about a whole family of bacteria, the cocci, use the word root _____ .

cocc

450

Pneumonia is caused by the pneumococcus. From this, you know that the germ responsible for pneumonia belongs to the family _____ / ____ (plural).

cocc/i
kok' si

451

One form of meningitis is caused by the meningococcus. It, too, is a member of the family

cocc/i

_____ / ____ (plural).

452

There are three main types of cocci.
Cocci growing in pairs are

Dipl / o /   /

Dipl/o/cocc/i

Cocci growing in twisted chains are

Strept / o /   /

Strept/o/cocc/i

Cocci growing in clusters are

Staphyl / o /   /

Staphyl/o/cocc/i

453

Strept/o means twisted. Streptococci grow in twisted chains like this 〰〰. If you should see a chain of cocci when examining a slide under the microscope, you would say they were

strept/o/cocc/i

/ /   /

454

A particular infection is caused by a particular streptococcus.
Sore throat is caused by

Strept / o / cocc / us   epidemicus.

Some pus formation is due to

Strept/o/cocc/us

/ /   /   pyogenes.

Focal infections contain

Strept/o/cocc/us

/ /   /   viridans.

455

"Staphyle" is the Greek word for **bunch of grapes.** Staphyl/o is used to build words which suggest a bunch of grapes. Staphylococci grow in clusters like a bunch of _____.

grapes

456

Staphylococci grow in clusters like grapes. If you should see a cluster of cocci when using the microscope, you would say they were

staphyl/o/cocc/i
staf il o kok' si

/ /   /

457

The bacteria that cause carbuncles grow in a cluster like a bunch of grapes. Carbuncles are caused by

staphyl/o/cocc/i

/ /   /

458

Most bacteria that form pus grow in a cluster. They are _____.

staphylococci

459

A common form of food poisoning is also caused by _____.

staphylococci

460

At the back of the mouth, hanging like a bunch of grapes, is the uvula. To build words about the uvula you also use the word root–combining form that means **like a bunch of grapes.** This is

_____ / _____ .

staphyl/o

461

Surgical repair of the uvula is

_____ / _____ / _____ / _____ .

staphyl/o/plast/y
staphyloplasty
staf' i lo plas ti

462

Staphyl/itis means ** _____

_____ .

inflammation of the uvula

463

Staphyl/ectomy means ** _____

_____ .

excision of the uvula

464

Py/o is the word root–combining form used for words involving pus. A py/o/cele is a hernia con-taining _____ .

pus

465

Many staphylococci are pyogenic. Py/o/gen/ic means producing _____ .

pus

466

Py/orrhea means discharge of _____ .

pus

467

Py/o/thorax means an accumulation of pus in the thoracic cavity. When pus-forming bacteria invade the thoracic lining,

_____ / _____ / _____ results.

py/o/thorax
pyothorax
pi o tho' raks

468

Pyothorax may follow chest disease. Pneumonia is one chest disease that can result in

_____ .

pyothorax

469

Bronchopneumonia and bronchiectasis are two other diseases causing

pyothorax

_____.

470

A py/o/gen/ic bacterium is one that forms pus. You know the word "genesis" for formation or beginning. The adjective that means something that produces or forms pus is

py/o/gen/ic
pyogenic
pi o jen' ik

_____/_____/_____/_____.

471

Pyogenic bacteria are found in boils. Boils become purulent (contain pus). This pus is formed by

pyogenic

_____ bacteria.

472

One type of staphylococcus causes boils. Therefore, you can say these staphylococci are _____

pyogenic

bacteria.

473

orrhea is a combining form that you will use as a suffix. orrhea ends a word and it follows a word root. orrhea means flow or discharge. Py/orrhea means

discharge of pus

** _____.

474

py/orrhea
pyorrhea
pi o re' a

orrhea refers to any flow or discharge. A discharge or flow of pus is called _____.

475

Pyorrhea alveolaris is a disease of the teeth and gums. The part of this disease's name that tells you that pus is discharged is

pyorrhea

_____.

476

There is also a disease of the salivary gland symptomized by the flow of pus. This is _____

pyorrhea

_____ salivaris.

477

Ot/orrhea means a discharging ear. Ot/o is the word root–combining form for _____.

ear

478

Ot/orrhea is both a symptom and a disease. No matter which is meant, the word

ot/orrhea
otorrhea
o to re' a

_____/_____ is used.

479

The disease, otorrhea, involves discharge, inflammation, and deafness. One of the symptoms of this disease is found in its name,

otorrhea

_____.

480

Otorrhea may be caused by ot/itis media. Ot/itis means

inflammation of the ear

** _____.

481

Otitis usually causes **ear pain,** which in medical terminology we call _____/___/_____/_____

otodynia
ot o din i' a or
otalgia
o tal' ji a

or _____/_____.

482

When otorrhea is established as a disease, there has been enough destruction of the tissue that

otodynia or
otalgia

_____ (ear pain) no longer occurs.

483

Small children often complain of earache. Medically, this could be called

otodynia or
otalgia

_____.

484

Rhinorrhea means discharge from the nose. Rhin/o is used in words about the _____.

nose

485

Using what is necessary from rhin/o, form a word that means inflammation of the nose:

rhin/itis
rhinitis
ri ni' tis

_____/_____.

486

Rhin/orrhea is a symptom. Drainage from the nose due to a head cold is a symptom called

rhin/orrhea
rhinorrhea
ri no re' a

_____.

487

A discharge from the sinuses through the nose is a form of _____.

rhinorrhea

488

Nasal catarrh is another source of

rhinorrhea

_____.

489

Build a word that means surgical repair of the nose:

rhin/o/plast/y
rhinoplasty
ri' no plas ti

_____ / _____ / _____ / ____.

490

Form a word that means incision of the nose:

rhin/otomy
rhinotomy
ri not' o mi

_____ / _____.

491

A rhin/o/lith is a calculus or stone in the nose.
Lith/o is the combining form for

calculus
or stone

** ** _____.

492

Lithogenesis means producing or forming

calculi (calculus)
or stones

** ** _____.

493

Lithology is the science of dealing with or studying

calculi
or stones

_____.

494

Using what is necessary from lith/o, build a word
meaning: an incision for the removal of a stone

lith/otomy
lithotomy
lith ot' o mi
lithometer
(You pronounce)

_____ / _____; an instrument

for measuring size of calculi

_____ / ____ / _____.

495

Calculi or stones can be formed many places in
the body. A chol/e/lith is a gallstone. Chol/e is the

gall or bile

word root–combining form for _____.

496

Chol/e/lith means gallstone. One cause of gallbladder disease is the presence of a gallstone or

chol/e/lith
cholelith
ko' le lith

_____ / ____ / _____.

497

A cholelith may be large or small. Regardless of

cholelith

size, the very presence of any _____
indicates a diseased gallbladder.

498

No matter what the size or shape, irritation and blockage of the gallbladder can be caused by a

cholelith

_____ .

499

Gall is secreted by the gallbladder. Chol/e/cyst is a medical name for the

gallbladder

_____ .

500

Gallstones can result in inflammation of the gallbladder (chol/e/cyst). Medically, this is called

chol/e/cyst/itis
cholecystitis
ko le sis ti' tis

_____ / ___ / _____ / _____ .

501

Cholecystitis is accompanied by pain and hyperemesis. Fatty foods aggravate these symptoms and should be avoided in cases of

cholecystitis

_____ .

502

Butter, cream, and even whole milk contain fat and should be avoided by patients with

cholecystitis

_____ .

503

chol/e/cyst/otomy
cholecystotomy
ko le sis tot' o mi
or
chol/e/lith/otomy
cholelithotomy
kol e lith ot' o mi

When a cholelith causes cholecystitis, one of two surgical procedures may be needed. One is an incision into the gallbladder, a

_____ / ___ / _____ / _____ .

504

chol/e/cyst/ectomy
cholecystectomy
ko le sis tekt' o mi

Usually the presence of a gallstone calls for the excision of the gallbladder. This is a

_____ / ___ / _____ / _____ .

505

rhin/o/lith
rhinolith
ri' no lith

A calculus or stone in the nose is a

_____ / ___ / _____ .

506

On the next page, you will find additional material to help you with word building. The chances are fifty-fifty that by now you have figured out a system concerning the order in which word parts go together. If you have, you may skip the next page. If you have not, study the next page; it will help you.

RULE I: About 90 per cent of the time, the part of the word that is indicated first comes last.

Examples

1. Inflammation of the bladder

inflammation		/	itis
(of the) bladder	cyst	/	
	cyst	/	itis

2. One who specializes in skin disorders

one who specializes (studies)		/ /	logist
(in) skin (disorders)	dermat	/o/	
	dermat	/o/	logist

3. Pertaining to the abdomen and bladder

pertaining to		/ /		/	ic
(the) abdomen	abdomin	/o/		/	
(and) bladder		/ /	cyst	/	
	abdomin	/o/	cyst	/	ic

RULE II: Where body systems are involved, words are usually built in order of organs passed in going through the system. (The first part still comes last.)

Examples

1. Inflammation of the stomach and small intestine

inflammation		/ /		/	itis
(of the) stomach	gastr	/o/		/	
(and) small intestine		/ /	enter	/	
	gastr	/o/	enter	/	itis

2. Removal of the uterus, fallopian tubes, and ovaries

removal of		/ /		/ /		/	ectomy
(the) uterus	hyster	/o/		/ /		/	
fallopian tubes		/ /	salping	/o/		/	
(and) ovaries		/ /		/ /	-oophor	/	
	hyster	/o/	salping	/o/	-oophor	/	ectomy

Of course, prefixes still come in front of the word.

507

slow

brad/y is used in words to mean slow. Brad/y/cardi/a means _____ heart action.

508

brad/y/phag/ia
bradyphagia
brad i fa' ji a

Brad/y/phag/ia means slowness in eating. Abnormally slow swallowing is also called

_____ / _____ / _____ .

509

bradyphagia

From brad/y/phag/ia you find the word root **phag** for eat. (More of phag/o later.) Slow eating is

_____ .

510

bradyphagia

A child who plays with his food while eating is exhibiting

_____ .

511

slowness of movement

Kinesi/o is used in words to mean movement or motion. Brad/y/kinesi/a means ** _____

_____ .

512

pain on movement or
movement pain

Kinesi/algia means
**_____ .

513

kinesi/algia
kinesialgia
ki ne si al' ji a

Kinesi/algia occurs when you have to move any sore or injured part of the body. Moving a broken arm causes

_____ .

514

After one's first ride on horseback, almost any movement causes

kinesialgia

_____ .

515

kinesi/ology
kinesiology
kin es i ol' o ji

Ology is used like a suffix to mean **study of.** (Remember **ologist?**) The study of muscular movements

is _____ / _____ .

516

Kinesi/ology is the study of movement. The study of muscular movement during exercise would be done in the field of

kinesiology

_____ / _____ .

517

The whole science of how the body moves is embraced in the field of

kinesiology

_____ .

518

abnormally slow movement

Brad/y/kinesi/a means ** _____

_____ .

519

brad/y/cardi/a
bradycardia
brad i kar' di a

Abnormally slow heart action is

_____ / _____ / _____ / _____ .

520

Tach/y is used in words to show the opposite of slow. Tachy means ** _____ .

fast or rapid

521

Tach/y/cardi/a means

rapid heart action

** _____ .

522

tach/y/phag/ia
tachyphagia
tak i fa' ji a

The word for fast eating is

_____ / _____ / _____ / _____ .

523

Sports cars have a tach/y/meter that measures engine speed. The speed at which blood circulates is also measured by a

tachymeter
tak im' e ter

_____ .

524

tach/y/cardi/a
tachycardia
tak i kar' di a

An abnormally fast heartbeat is called

_____ / _____ / _____ / _____ .

525

Pne/o comes from the Greek word pneia, breathe.
Pne/o any place in a word means

breathe or breathing

_____ .

526

When pne/o begins a word, the "p" is silent. When pne/o occurs later in a word, it is pronounced. In

silent

pne/o/pne/ic the first "p" is _____ ;
the second is pronounced.

527

In pne/o/pne/ic, pne refers to

breathing or breathe

_____ .

63

528

slow breathing
tach/y/pne/a
tachypnea
tak ip ne' a

Brad/y/pne/a means ** _____
_____ . A word for rapid breathing is
_____ / ____ / _____ / _____ .

529

The rate of respiration (breathing) is controlled by the amount of carbon dioxide in the blood. Increased carbon dioxide speeds up breathing and

tachypnea

causes _____ .

530

Muscle exercise increases the amount of carbon dioxide in the blood. This speeds respiration and

tachypnea

produces _____ .

531

Running a race causes

tachypnea

_____ .

532

a is a prefix meaning **without.** Apnea literally means

without breathing

** _____ .

533

A/pnea **really** means temporary cessation of breathing. If the failure to breathe were not temporary, death would result rather than

a/pne/a
apnea
ap ne' a

_____ / _____ / _____ .

534

Apnea means temporary cessation of breathing. If the level of carbon dioxide in the blood falls

apnea

very low, _____ results.

535

apnea
brad/y/pne/a
bradypnea
brad ip ne' a

When breathing ceases for a bit, _____ results. If breathing is merely very slow, it is called
_____ / ____ / _____ / _____ .

536

a

The prefix meaning without is _____ .

537

without generation
(origin)

Genesis is both a Greek and an English word. It means generation (origin or beginning). A/genes/is means ** _____ .

538

By extention, agenesis means failure to develop or lack of development. When an organ does not develop, physicians use the word

a/genes/is
agenesis
a jen' e sis

_____/_____/_____ .

539

Agenesis can refer to any part of the body. If a hand does not develop, the condition is called

agenesis

_____ of the hand.

540

When the stomach is not formed, _____ of the stomach results.

agenesis

541

Dys/men/orrhea means painful menstruation. The prefix for painful, bad, or difficult is _____ .

dys

542

Dysphagia means difficult swallowing. Analyze

dys/phag/ia
dis fa' ji a

dysphagia: _____/_____/_____ .
dys in dysphagia means

difficult

_____ .

543

Dys/troph/y literally means bad development. The word for difficult breathing is

dys/pne/a
dyspnea
disp ne' a

_____/_____/_____ .

544

Pepsis is the Greek word for digestion. From this you get the word root–combining form peps/o to use in words about _____ .

digestion

545

Dys/peps/ia means poor _____ .
When food is eaten too rapidly,

digestion
dys/peps/ia
dyspepsia
dis pep' si a

_____/_____/_____ may result.

546

Dyspepsia is a noun. Eating under tension also causes _____ .

dyspepsia

547

Contemplating the troubles of the world when eating is a good cause for _____ .

dyspepsia

a/peps/ia   apepsia
a pep' si a
brad/y/peps/ia
bradypepsia
brad i pep' si a

548
Cessation of digestion (without digestion) is

_____ / _____ / _____, while slow digestion

is _____ / / _____ / _____ .

Work Review Sheets 6 and 7.

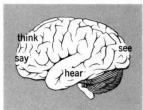

549
Refer to the chart on the next page when working Frames 550 through 563.

550
An embryonic (germ) cell from which a muscle cell develops is a **my/o/blast.**
A germ cell from which a nerve cell develops is a

neur/o/blast
nu' ro blast

_____ / / _____ .

angioblast
an' ji o blast

A germ cell from which vessels develop is an

_____ / / _____ .

551
A spasm of a nerve is a **neur/o/spasm.**

myospasm
mi' o spazm

A spasm of a muscle is a _____ / / _____ .
A spasm of a vessel is an

angi/o/spasm
an' ji o spazm

_____ / / _____ .

552
A (condition of) hardening of nerve tissue is **neur/o/scler/osis.**
A hardening of a vessel is

angi/o/scler/osis
an ji o skler o' sis

_____ / / _____ / _____ .

myosclerosis
mi o skler o' sis

A hardening of muscle tissue is

_____ / / _____ / _____ .

553
A tumor containing muscle fibers is a **my/o/fibr/oma.**
A tumor containing nerve fibers is a

neurofibroma
nu ro fi bro' ma

_____ / / _____ / _____ .

angi/o/fibr/oma
an ji o fi bro' ma

A vessel tumor containing fibers is an

_____ / / _____ / _____ .

COMBINING FORM	COMBINING FORM	SUFFIX
my/o (muscle)	spasm o/spasm/o (twitch, twitching)	spasm (word in itself)
	blast o/blast/o (germ or embryonic; gives rise to something else)	blast (word in itself)
angi/o (vessel)	scler/o (hard)	osis (use with scler/o)
	fibr/o (fibrous, fiber)	oma (use with fibr/o)
neur/o (nerve or neuron)	lys/o (breaking down, destruction)	is—noun suffix (use with lys/o)

554

The destruction of muscle tissue is **my/o/lys/is.**
The destruction of nerve tissue is

neur/o/lys/is
nu rol' is is

_____ / _____ / _____ .

The destruction or breaking down of vessels is

angi/o/lys/is
an ji ol' is is

_____ / _____ / _____ .

555

Arteri/o is used in words about the arteries. Arteries are blood vessels that carry blood away from the heart. A word meaning **hardening of the arteries is**

arteri/o/scler/osis
arteriosclerosis
ar te ri o skler o' sis

_____ / _____ / _____ .

556

Arteri/o/scler/osis means hardening of the arteries.
Build a word meaning:

a fibrous condition of the arteries

arteriofibrosis
ar te ri o fi bro' sis

_____ / _____ / _____ .

a softening of the arteries

arteriomalacia
ar te ri o ma la' ci a

_____ / _____ / _____ .

557
Give a word for:
arterial spasm

_____/____/_____.

gastric spasm

_____/____/_____.

softening of the stomach walls

_____/____/_____/_____.

arteriospasm
ar te' ri o spazm

gastrospasm
gas' tro spazm

gastromalacia
gas tro mal a' ci a

558
Build a word meaning:
destruction (breakdown) of fat

_____/____/_____/_____.

destruction (breakdown) of cells

_____/____/_____/_____.

destruction of blood tissue

hem   /o/   /_____.

lip/o/lys/is
lip ol' is is

cyt/o/lys/is
ci tol' is is

hem/o/lys/is
hem ol' is is

559
Hem/o refers to blood. A tumor of a blood vessel
is a hem/angi/oma. (Note dropped **o**.)
An inflammation of a blood vessel is

_____/_____/_____.

A condition of blood in a joint is

_____/_____/_____.

hemangiitis
hem an ji i' tis

hemarthrosis
hem ar thro' sis

560
Hemat/o also refers to blood.
Another word for destruction of blood tissue is

_____/____/_____/_____.

An abnormal fear of blood is

_____/____/_____/_____.

hemat/o/lys/is
hem at ol' is is

hemat/o/phob/ia
hem at o fo' bi a

561
Still use hemat/o to mean _____.
The study of blood is

_____/____/_____/_____.

One who specializes in the science of blood is a

_____/____/_____/_____.

blood

hemat/o/log/y
hem at ol' o gi

hemat/o/log/ist
hem at ol' o gist

origin
formation of spermatozoa
or *origin*
formation of sperm
or *origin*
formation of male germ
cell

562

Sperma is the Greek word meaning seed. Spermat/o is used in words about spermat/o/zoa or male germ cell (sperm). Spermat/o/genesis means
** _____

_____ .

563

Give a word meaning:
    the destruction of spermatozoa

spermat/o/lys/is
sper mat ol' is is
    /   /   /
_____ .

    an embryonic male cell

spermat/o/blast
sper mat' o blast
       /   /
_____ .

564

A bladder or sac containing sperm is a

spermat/o/cyst
sper mat' o sist
       /   /
_____ .

A word for resembling sperm is

spermat/oid
sper' mat oyd
           /
_____ .

A word for disease of sperm is

spermat/o/path/y
sper mat op' a thi
       /   /   /
_____ .

565

Summarize what you learned in Frames 550 to 564.

muscle	my/o	means _____ .
vessel	angi/o	means _____ .
nerve	neur/o	means _____ .

566

twitching	spasm	means _____ .
germ or embryonic	blast/o	means _____ .
hard	scler/o	means _____ .
fibrous	fibr/o	means _____ .
destruction	lys/o	means _____ .

567

spermatozoa (sperm)	spermat/o	means _____ .
blood	hemat/o	means _____ .
blood	hem/o	means _____ .
formation *origin*	genesis	means _____ .

568

The Greek word for egg is oon. In scientific words, o/o (pronounce both o's) means egg or ovum. An o/o/blast is
** _____

an embryonic egg cell
(a cell that will
become an ovum)

69

569

o/o/genesis
oogenesis
o o gen' e sis

O/o/genesis is the formation and development of an ovum. The changes that occur in the cell from ooblast to mature ovum are

_____ / _____ / _____.

570

oogenesis

Oogenesis must be complete for the ovum to be mature. It is impossible for a spermatozoon to fertilize an ovum until _____
is complete.

571

oogenesis

In fact, an ovum is not even discharged from the ovary until after the completion of

_____.

572

ovary

The word root–combining form used in words that refer to the ovary is oophor/o. When you see oophor in a word, you think of the _____.

573

ovary

The ovary is the organ that is responsible for maturing and discharging the ovum. About every 28 days an ovum is discharged from the

_____.

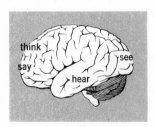

574

This frame shows the development of oophorectomy:

o/o		egg	from Greek, oon
phor/o		bear	from Greek, phoros
ect/o		out	from Greek, ektos
tom/y	cut	from Greek, tomos

This is included for those who are interested.

575

excision of the ovary

Oophor/o is used in words to refer to the ovary. Oophorectomy means
** _____.

576

Using what you need from oophor/o, build a word that means:

inflammation of an ovary

_____/_____.

excision of an ovary

_____/_____.

tumor of an ovary
(ovarian tumor)

_____/_____.

oophor/itis oophoritis
o of o ri' tis
oophor/ectomy
oophorectomy
o of o rek' to me
oophor/oma oophoroma
o of o ro' ma

577

Oophoropexy means fixation of a displaced ovary. Pex/o is a word root–combining form that means

_____.

fixation

578

An oophor/o/pex/y is a surgical procedure. When an ovary is displaced, an

_____/_____/_____/_____ is per-

formed.

oophor/o/pex/y
oophoropexy
o of' o ro pek si

579

Oophoropexy is a noun. You can see the noun suf-fix "y" ending the word

_____/_____/_____/_____.

oophoropexy

580

The surgical procedure for a prolapsed (dropped or sagged) ovary is called an

_____.

oophoropexy

581

Salping/o is used to build words that refer to the fallopian tube(s). A salpingoscope is an instrument used to examine the

*_____.

fallopian tube(s)

582

A salpingostomy is a surgical opening into a

*_____.

fallopian tube

583

Using what you need of salping/o, build a word meaning:

inflammation of a fallopian tube

_____ / _____

excision of a fallopian tube

_____ / _____

salping/itis
salpingitis
sal pin ji' tis
salping/ectomy
salpingectomy
sal pin jek' to me

584

When building compound medical words, if two like vowels occur between word roots or combining forms they are separated by a hyphen. For a model use **salpingo-oophorectomy,** and build a word that means inflammation of the fallopian tube and ovary:

_____ / _____ / _____ / _____ .

salping/o-/oophor/itis
salpingo-oophoritis
sal ping go-o o for i' tis

585

A hernia that encloses the ovary and fallopian tube is a

_____ / _____ / _____ / _____ .

salping/o-/oophor/o/cele
salpingo-oophorocele
sal ping go-o of' or o sel

586

In words built from laryng/o, pharyng/o, salping/o, and mening/o, the "g" is pronounced as a hard "g" when followed by an "o" or an "a." The "g" in **good** is a hard "g."

explanation for next
frame

587

In laryngalgia and salpingocele, the "g" of the word root is pronounced hard as in good. In pharyngalgia and meningocele, the word root "g" also is given a _____ pronunciation.

hard
(Pronounce them)

588

In laryngostomy, pharyngotomy, salpingopexy, and meningomalacia, the "g" is given a _____ sound.

hard
(Pronounce them)

589

A hard "g" precedes the vowels _____ and _____ .

o and a

590

In words built from laryng/o, pharyng/o, salping/o, and mening/o, the "g" is soft when followed by an "e" or an "i." The "g" in **germ** and **giant** is soft.

explanation for next
frame

591

soft
(Pronounce them)

In laryngectomy and salpingitis, the "g" is a soft "g" as in germ. In meningeal and pharyngitis, the "g" also is given a _____ pronunciation.

592

soft
(Pronounce them)

In meningitis, salpingian, laryngitis, and pharyngectomy, the "g" is given a _____ sound.

593

e and i

A soft "g" precedes the vowels ____ and ____.

594

a and o
e and i

"g" is given a hard sound when followed by the vowels ____ and ____. "g" is given the soft "j" sound when followed by the vowels ____ and ____.

595

two like vowels join word roots or combining forms

In compound words a hyphen (-) is used when
** _____.

596

information frame

The spermatozoon is the male germ cell. The ovum is the female egg cell. When they unite in the fallopian tube, a new life begins. The fertilized ovum moves into the uterus where it is incubated until birth.

597

uterus

Hyster/o is used to build words about the uterus. A hyster/ectomy is an excision of the

_____.

598

uterus

A hysterotomy is an incision into the _____,

uterus

and a hysterospasm is a spasm of the

_____.

599

hyster/o/path/y
hysteropathy
his ter op' ath i

Hyster/o/pex/y means surgical fixation of the uterus. Any uterine disease is called

_____ / ____ / _____ / ____ .

73

600

A hyster/o/salping/o-/oophor/ectomy is the excision of the uterus, fallopian tubes, and ovaries. Analyze this word:

hyster/o

_____/ combining form for uterus.

salping/o

_____/ combining form for fallopian tubes.

oophor

_____ word root for ovary.

ectomy

_____ suffix—excision.

hyster/o/salping/o-/
   oophor/ectomy
hysterosalpingo-
   oophorectomy
his ter o sal pin go-
oo for ek' to mi

601

Build the word that means excision of the uterus, fallopian tubes, and ovaries.

_____/____/_____/____/_____/_____

602

A word meaning fixation of the uterus is

hyster/o/pex/y
hysteropexy
his' ter o peks i

_____/____/_____/_____. A

word meaning uterine hernia is

hyster/o/cele
hysterocele
his' ter o sel

_____/____/_____.

603

Hyster/o/ptosis means prolapse of the uterus. Ptosis is a word that means

prolapse

_____.

604

Hysteroptosis is a compound word constructed from:

hyster/o

_____/ the combining form for uterus.

ptosis
to' sis

_____ a word meaning prolapse.

605

When prolapse occurs, a fixation is usually done. A hysteropexy would be done to correct or repair

hyster/o/ptosis
hysteroptosis
his ter op to' sis

_____/____/_____.

606

Many organs can prolapse or sag. When the uterus prolapses, it is called

hysteroptosis
his ter op to' sis

_____/____/_____.

74

607

When the broad ligament that helps support the uterus weakens,

hysteroptosis _____/____/_____

can occur.

608

Blephar/o/ptosis means prolapse of an eyelid. The word root–combining form for eyelid is

blephar/o _____/_____.

609

Blepharedema means swelling of the

eyelid _____.

Blephar/o seen anywhere makes you think of the

eyelid _____.

610

Blephar/edema means swelling of the eyelid. Build a word that means:

    inflammation of an eyelid

blepharitis
blef ar i' tis _____/_____

    incision of an eyelid

blepharotomy
blef ar ot' o mi _____/_____

611

Build a word that means:

    surgical repair of eyelid

blepharoplasty
blef' ar o plas ti _____/____/_____/____

    twitching of an eyelid

blepharospasm
blef' ar o spazm _____/____/_____

    prolapse of an eyelid

blepharoptosis
blef ar op to' sis _____/____/_____

Work Review Sheets 8 and 9.

612

nephr/o/ptosis
nephroptosis
nef rop to' sis

Nephr/o is used in words to refer to the kidney. A word that means prolapse of the kidney is

_____/____/_____.

613

Nephr/o/ptosis can occur from a hard blow or jolt. Men who ride motorcycles wear special clothing or a kidney belt to protect against

nephroptosis _____.

75

614

Nephritis means

inflammation of a kidney

** _____.

Build a word meaning:

fixation of a kidney

nephr/o/pex/y
nephropexy
nef' ro peks i
nephrolysis
nef rol' is is

_____ / ___ / _____ / ____

destruction of kidney tissue

_____ / ___ / _____ / ____

615

Build a word meaning:

stone in the kidney

nephrolith
nef' ro lith

_____ / ___ / ____

softening of kidney tissue

nephromalacia
nef ro ma la' si a

_____ / ___ / _____ / ____

enlargement of the kidney

nephromegaly
nef ro meg' a li

_____ / ___ / _____ / ____

616

In your dictionary, find a drawing of the **ur**inary tract. The **ur**inary tract is responsible for forming **ur**ine from waste materials in the blood, and eliminating **ur**ine from the body. What would you guess

ur

to be the word root for **ur**ine? _____.

617

From the picture in the dictionary identify these parts:

kidney	—forms urine
renal pelvis	—collects urine in the kidney
ureter	—carries urine to the bladder
bladder	—stores urine until voiding
urethra	—discharges urine from the body

618

On the next page is some information to help you work Frames 619 to 634. While learning terminology related to the urinary tract refer to this information as well as the picture in your dictionary.

619

renal pelvis

Pyel/o refers to the *_____.

WORD	WORD ROOT–COMBINING FORM	NEW SUFFIX TO USE WHEN NEEDED*
urine	ur/o	
kidney	nephr/o	orrhaphy (suturing or stitching)
renal pelvis	pyel/o	
ureter	ureter/o	orrhagia (hemorrhage or "bursting forth" of blood)
bladder	cyst/o	
urethra	urethr/o	

* **Note:** These two involved combining forms that can be used as suffixes start with **orrh.** You have now learned three of the four **rrh** "suffixes."

620

Using what you need from the combining form for renal pelvis, form words meaning:

pyel/itis
pi el i' tis

    inflammation of the renal pelvis

_____/_____

pyel/o/plast/y
pi' el o plas ti

    surgical repair of the renal pelvis

_____/____/_____/_____

621

condition of renal
pelvis and kidney

Pyel/o/nephr/osis means ** _____

_____. Form a word

pyel/o/nephr/itis
pi el o nef ri' tis

that means inflammation of the renal pelvis and kidney. _____

622

stone or calculus in
the ureter

Ureter/o/lith means

    ** _____.

Form a word that means:

    herniation of the ureter

ureter/o/cele
u re' ter o sel
ureteropathy
u re ter op' a thi

_____/____/_____

    any disease of the ureter

_____/____/_____/_____

623

plastic surgery of the
ureter and renal pelvis

Ureter/o/pyel/o/plast/y means ** _____

_____.

Form a word meaning inflammation of the ureter and renal pelvis.

ureter/o/pyel/itis
ureteropyelitis
u re ter o pi el i' tis

_____/____/_____/_____

624

Form a word meaning:
    making a new opening between the ureter and bladder

ureter/o/cyst/ostomy
u re ter o sis tos' to mi

_____ / / _____ / _____

a condition of the ureter involving pus

ureteropyosis
u re ter o pi o' sis

_____ / / _____ / _____

625

Ureter/orrhaphy introduces a new word part. **or-rhaphy** is not really a suffix, but again (for simplification) it can be used as one. orrhaphy means

suturing or stitching

** _____ .

626

Form the word that means suturing of the ureter.

ureter/orrhaphy
ureterorrhaphy
u re ter or' ra fi

_____ / _____

627

Form a word meaning:
    suturing of a kidney

nephr/orrhaphy
nephrorrhaphy
nef ror' a fi
cyst/orrhaphy
cystorrhaphy
sist or' a fi

_____ / _____

suture of the bladder

_____ / _____

628

Form a word meaning:
    suture of a nerve

neur/orrhaphy
nu ror' a fi

_____ / _____

suturing of the eyelids

blephar/orrhaphy
blef a ror' raf i

_____ / _____

629

carries urine from the body or removes urine from the bladder

The urethra is the organ that ** _____
_____ . The word root-combining form for urethra is

urethr/o

_____ / __ .

630

Urethr/orrhaphy means
** _____ .

Form a word meaning:
    incision into the urethra
_____
            /

    spasm of the urethra
_____
       /   /

suturing of the urethra

urethr/otomy
u re throt' o mi

urethr/o/spasm
u re' thro spazm

631

Urethr/o/rect/al means pertaining to the urethra and rectum. Urethr/o/vagin/al means pertaining to the _____ and vagina. Form a word that means inflammation of urethra and bladder.
_____
      /   /   /

urethra

urethr/o/cyst/itis
urethrocystitis
u re thro sis ti' tis

632

orrhagia is another complex word part that can be used as a suffix because it follows a word root and ends a word. orrhagia means ** _____
_____ .

hemorrhage or bursting forth of blood

633

Gastr/orrhagia means stomach hemorrhage. Encephal/orrhagia means brain _____ .
A word that means hemorrhage of the urethra is
_____
         / .

hemorrhage
urethr/orrhagia
urethrorrhagia
u re thror a' ji a

634

Build a word meaning:
    hemorrhage of the bladder
_____
       /

    hemorrhage of the ureter
_____
       /

cyst/orrhagia
sist or ra' ji a

ureter/orrhagia
u re ter or ra' ji a

635

Pne/o refers to breathing. The lungs are the organs of the body that take in air (breathe). **Pneu**mon/o is used in medical words concerning lungs. Pneumon/ectomy means
** _____ .

excision of lungs

79

Pneumon/o/path/y means

** _____ .

any disease of the lungs
pneumon/orrhagia
pneumonorrhagia
nu mon or ra' ji a

Form a word meaning hemorrhage of a lung.

/ _____

637

Pneumon/ia is a disease of the lungs. Read about pneumonia in your dictionary, then fill the next two frames on the basis of this information.

free fun frame

638

In general you can say:

is

Pneumonia _____ (is/is not) a serious disease.

should not

Patients with pneumonia _____ (should/should not) talk much.

are

Penicillin and sulfonamides _____ (are/ are not) the drugs most used to treat pneumonia.

terminal pneumonia
(If you missed this, don't worry. Just read this again and THINK.)

639

The most serious form of pneumonia is

_____ .

640

Virus pneumon/ia is called pneumonitis. Two acceptable ways of saying that the patient has a virus infection of lung tissue is to use the word

pneumon/itis
nu mo ni' tis
pneumon/ia
nu mo' ni a

/ _____ or to say

virus _____ / _____ .

641

Pneumon/o/melan/osis is a lung disease in which lung tissue becomes black due to breathing black dust. The word root for black is _____ .

melan

642

Pneumon/o/melan/osis literally means a condition of black lungs. Analyze this word:

pneumon/o

_____ / ___ combining form for lung

melan

_____ word root for black

osis

_____ suffix—condition

643

pneumon/o/melan/osis
pneumonomelanosis
nu mo no mel an o' sis

Construct a word meaning condition of lung black-ness:

_____ / _____ / _____ / _____.

644

pneumon/o/melan/osis

The inhalation (breathing) of black dust results in

_____ / _____ / _____.

pneumonomelanosis

The inhalation of much soot or black smoke can also cause _____.

645

black

Melan/o means _____.
Melan/osis means black pigmentation. A word that means black tumor is

melan/oma
melanoma
mel an o' ma

_____ / _____.

646

melan/o/cyte
melanocyte
mel' a no site

Melan/in is the pigment which gives dark color to the hair, skin, and choroid of the eye. A black pig-mented cell is a

_____ / _____ / _____.

647

black or dark skin
coloring (pigmentation)
(literally—black skin)

Melanoderma means
**

_____.

648

melan/o/carcin/oma
melanocarcinoma
mel a no kar sin o' ma

You have already learned that a carcin/oma is a form of cancer. A darkly pigmented cancer is

_____ / _____ / _____.

649

Whenever any hairless mole on the skin turns black and grows, a physician should be consulted, for there is possible danger of black-mole cancer or

melanocarcinoma

_____ / _____ / _____.

650

Pneumon/o/myc/osis means a fungus disease of the lungs. The word root that means "fungus" is

myc

_____.

81

651

fungus (singular)
fun' gus
fungi (plural)
fun' ji

Myc/o seen any place in a word should make you think of _____ .

652

pl.   *singular*

fungi or fungus

In high school biology, you read or even learned the words **myc**elium and **myc**elial. Myc refers to

_____ .

653

pneumon/o/myc/osis
pneumonomycosis
nu mo no mi ko' sis

A mycosis is any condition caused by a fungus. A condition of lung fungus is

_____ / _____ / _____ / _____ .

654

myc/oid
mi' koyd
myc/o/log/y
mycology
mi kol' o ji

Build a word meaning:

resembling fungi _____ / _____

study of fungi _____ / _____ / _____

655

Build a word meaning:

fungus disease (condition) of the pharynx

_____ pharyng /o/ _____ / _____

pharyngomycosis
rhinomycosis
dermatomycosis
(Try to pronounce them yourself)

fungus disease (condition) of the nose

_____ / _____ / _____

fungus disease of the skin

_____ / _____ / _____

656

Pneum/o and pneumon/o can both refer to the lung. Pneum/o is derived from the Greek word "pneuma" (air). Pneum/o is used in words to mean air.

657

lung or lungs

Pneum/o comes from the Greek word "pneumon" (lung). Pneumon/o is used only in words that refer to the _____ .

658

air

Pneum/o comes from the Greek word "pneuma" (air). Pneum/o is used in most words to mean _____ but can also be used to mean lung.

82

659

Your use of pneum/o will be in words about air. Pneum/o/derm/a means a collection of air under the skin. A collection of air in the chest cavity (thorax) is a

pneum/o/thorax
pneumothorax
nu mo tho' raks

_____ / _____ / _____ .

660

The word root–combining form for thorax (chest cavity) is _____ / _____ . The adjective that pertains to a collection of air in the chest cavity is

thorac/o

pneum/o/thorac/ic
pneumothoracic

_____ / _____ / _____ / _____ .

661

Hydrotherapy means treatment with water. Treatment with compressed air is called

pneum/o/therap/y
pneumotherapy
nu mo ther' a pi

_____ / _____ / _____ / _____ .

662

A tach/y/meter measures speed of any body in motion. An instrument that measures air volume in respiration is a

pneum/o/meter
nu mom' et er

_____ / _____ / _____ .

663

A collection of air and serum in the chest cavity is pneum/o/ser/o/thorax. A collection of air and pus in the thoracic cavity is a

pneumopyothorax
pneumohemothorax
(hemat/o/)
(You try the pronunciation yourself)

_____ / _____ / _____ / _____ / _____ ,

while a collection of air and blood in this same cavity is a

_____ / _____ / _____ / _____ / _____ .

Work Review Sheets 10 and 11.

664

On the next page is information to be used in building words through Frame 711. Open your dictionary or an anatomy book to the drawing of the digestive system, so you can see the organs to which the words refer. Refer to this drawing as well as the information on the next page. Food passes through the digestive system in the order of the organs listed on the next page.

ORGAN	WORD ROOT COMBINING FORM FOR ORGAN	ANOTHER WORD ROOT OR COMBINING FORM
mouth	stomat/o	
teeth	dent/o	
tongue	gloss/o	clysis—washing or irrigation
lips	cheil/o _philo_	(word in itself)
gums	gingiv/o	
esophagus	esophag/o	
stomach	gastr/o	
small intestine	enter/o	ectasia—dilatation or stretching (word in itself)
duodenum (1st part)	duoden/o	
jejunum (2nd part)	jejun/o	
ileum (3rd part)	ile/o	

		combining form	suffix
large intestine or colon	col/o	scop/o (examine)	e—noun (instrument) y—noun (process or action) ic—adjective
rectum	rect/o		

		combining form	suffix
anus and rectum	proct/o	pleg/a (paralysis)	ia—noun ic—adjective

glands of digestion liver pancreas	hepat/o pancreat/o	

665

The word root–combining form for mouth is

stomat/o
_____ / _____ .

666

Stomat/itis means
inflammation of the mouth
**
_____ .

surgical repair of the mouth

Stomat/o/plast/y means
**
_____ .

667

Using the word root for mouth, form a word meaning:

pain in the mouth

_____ / _____

stomat/algia
sto mat al' ji a

hemorrhage of the mouth

_____ / _____

stomat/orrhagia
sto ma tor ra' ji a

668

Using the combining form for mouth, build a word meaning:

condition of mouth fungus

_____ / ____ / _____ / _____

stomat/o/myc/osis
sto ma to mi ko' sis

any disease of the mouth

_____ / ____ / _____ / _____

stomat/o/path/y
sto ma top' a thi

669

A micr/o/scop/e is an instrument for examining something small. An instrument for examining the mouth is a

_____ / ____ / _____ / ____. The

stomat/o/scop/e
sto' mat o skop

process of examining with this instrument is

_____ / ____ / _____ / y __.

stomat/o/scop/y
sto ma tos' kop e

670

The word root–combining form for tongue is

_____ / _____.

gloss/o

Gloss/itis means
                  ** _____.

inflammation of the tongue

Gloss/ectomy means
                  ** _____.

excision of the tongue

671

Using the word root, build a word meaning:

pain in the tongue

_____ / _____

gloss/algia
glos sal' ji a
gloss/al
glossal
glos' sal

pertaining to the tongue

_____ / al _____

672

under the tongue or
to the tongue

One of the cranial nerves is the hypo/gloss/al. It supplies nerve impulses *_____ _____. A medication which is administered under the tongue is

hypo/gloss/al
hi po glos' sal

_____/_____/_____ medi-

cation.

673

Using the combining form for tongue, build a word meaning:

prolapse of the tongue

gloss/o/ptosis
gloss op' to sis

_____/___/_____

examination of the tongue

gloss/o/scop/y
gloss os' kop e

_____/___/_____/___

674

Using the information needed from page 84 build a word meaning:

paralysis of the tongue

gloss/o/pleg/ia
glos so ple' ji a

_____/___/_____/___
noun

glossoplegic
glos so ple' jic

paralysis of the tongue

_____/___/_____/___
adjective

675

inflammation of the lips

Cheil/itis means
**_____.

plastic surgery of the lips

Cheil/o/plast/y means
**_____.

676

cheil

cheil/o *kilo*

The word root for lip is _____. The combining form for lip is _____/___.

677

Build a word meaning:

incision of the lips

cheil/otomy
ki lot' o mi

_____/_____

cheil/osis
ki lo' sis

abnormal condition or morbid condition of the

lips _____/_____

678

A word meaning plastic surgery of the lips and mouth is

cheil/o/stomat/o/plast/y
cheilostomatoplasty
ki lo sto mat' o plas te

_____ / _____ / _____ / _____ / _____ .
lip .... mouth .... repair ... suffix

679

Gingiv/al means
 ** _____ .

pertaining to the gums

The word root–combining form for gums is
 _____ / _____ .

gingiv/o

680

Build a word meaning:

gingiv/itis
jin ji vi' tis
gingiv/algia
jin ji val' ji a

    inflammation of the gums
 _____ / _____

    gum pain _____ / _____

681

Build a word meaning:

gingiv/ectomy
gingivectomy
jin ji vek' to mi

    excision of gum tissue
 _____ / _____

gingiv/o/gloss/itis
(You pronounce it.)

    inflammation of the gums and tongue
 _____ / _____ / _____

682

Gastr/orrhagia means
 ** _____ .

stomach hemorrhage

Gastr/itis means
 ** _____ .

inflammation of the stomach

Gastr/ic means
 ** _____ .

pertaining to the stomach

683

Form a word meaning:

gastr/ectasia
gas trec' ta si a

    dilatation (stretching) of the stomach
 _____ / _____

gastr/o/enter/o/ptosis
gas tro en ter op to' sis

    prolapse of the stomach and small intestine
 _____ / _____ / _____ / _____

684

Form a word meaning:

gastr/o/enter/ic
gas tro en ter' ic

    pertaining to the stomach and small intestine
 _____ / _____ / _____

enter/orrhagia
en ter or ra' ji a

    hemorrhage of the small intestine
 _____ / _____

685

Build a word meaning:
   intestinal hernia

enter/o/cele
en' ter o sel
enter/o/clysis
enteroclysis
en ter ok' li sis

_____ / _____ / _____

washing or irrigation of the small intestine
_____ / _____ / _____

686

Build a word meaning:
   paralysis of the small intestine

enter/o/pleg/ia
en ter o ple' ji a

_____ / _____ / _____ / _____

enter/ectasia
en ter ec' ta si a

dilatation of the small intestine
_____ / _____

687

prolapse of the small
  intestine

Enter/o/ptosis means
     **
_____.

puncture of the small
  intestine

Enter/o/centesis means
     **
_____.

688

pertaining to the colon
  or large intestine

Col/ic means
**
_____.

puncture of the colon

Col/o/centesis means
     **
_____.

689

col/o/pex/y
colopexy
ko' lo pek si
col/ostomy
colostomy
ko los' to mi

Build a word meaning:
   surgical fixation of the colon

_____ / _____ / _____ / _____

making a new opening into the colon
_____ / _____

690

Build a word meaning:
   washing or irrigation of the colon

col/o/clysis
ko lok' li sis

_____ / _____ / _____

col/o/ptosis
ko lop to' sis

prolapse of the colon
_____ / _____ / _____

691

The combining form for small intestine is

_____/_____.

The combining form for large intestine (colon) is

_____/_____.

An instrument to examine the small intestine is the

_____/_____/_____/_____.

enter/o

col/o

enter/o/scop/e
en' ter o skōp

692

The word root–combining form for rectum is

_____/_____.

Rect/al means
**_____.

A rect/o/cele is
   **_____.

rect/o

pertaining to the rectum

a rectal hernia or hernia
of the rectum

693

Build a word meaning:
   washing or irrigation of the rectum
   _____/_____/_____

   instrument for examining the rectum
   _____/_____/_____/_____

rect/o/clysis
rek tok' lis is

rect/o/scop/e
rek' to skop

694

The process of examining the rectum with a recto-
scope is called

_____/_____/_____/_____.

In doing this, the physician has performed a

_____/_____/_____/_____
                          adjective

examination.

rect/o/scop/y
rek tos' ko pi

rectoscopic
rek to skop' ic

695

Build a word meaning:
   plastic surgery of the rectum
   _____/_____/_____/_____

   suturing (stitching) of the rectum
   _____/_____

rectoplasty
rek' to plas ti

rect/orrhaphy
rek tor' ra fi

696
Build a word meaning:
    pertaining to the rectum and urethra
_____ / ___ / _____ / _____

rect/o/urethr/al
rek to u re' thral

    incision of the bladder through the rectum
_____ / ___ / _____ / _____

rect/o/cyst/otomy
rek to sis tot' o mi

rectum   bladder   incision

697
A proct/o/log/ist is one who ** _____
_____ . Proct/
o/log/y is
    ** _____ .

specializes in diseases
    of anus and rectum

study of diseases of
    anus and rectum

698
Build a word meaning:
    washing or irrigation of anus and rectum
_____ / ___ / _____

proct/o/clysis
prok tok' li sis

    paralysis of the opening from the anus
_____ / ___ / _____ / _____

proct/o/pleg/ia or
proctoparalysis

699
A proctologist examines the rectum with a
_____ / ___ / _____ / _____ . This
examination is called
_____ / ___ / _____ / _____ .

proct/o/scop/e
prok' to skop

proct/o/scop/y
prok tos' ko pi

700
Build a word meaning:
    suturing of the rectum and anus
_____ / _____

    surgical fixation of the rectum
_____ / ___ / _____ / _____

proct/orrhaphy
prok tor' a fi
proct/o/pex/y
prok' to peks i
or
rect/o/pex/y

701
Hepat/ic means
    ** _____ .
Hepatomegaly means
    ** _____ .

pertaining to the liver

enlargement of the liver

702
Build a word meaning:
    inspection (examination) of the liver
_____ / ___ / _____ / _____

    any disease of the liver
_____ / ___ / _____ / _____

hepat/o/scop/y
hep a tos kop e

hepat/o/path/y
hep a top' a thi

703

Build a word meaning:
    incision into the liver

_____/_____

    excision of (part of) the liver

_____/_____

hepat/otomy
hep a tot' o mi

hepat/ectomy
hep a tek' to mi

704

Pancreat/ic means
        **
_____.

Pancreat/o/lys/is means **_____

_____.

pertaining to the pancreas

destruction of pancreatic tissue

705

Build a word meaning:
    a stone or calculus in the pancreas

_____/_____/_____

    any pancreatic disease

_____/_____/_____ _____/

pancreat/o/lith
pan kre at' o lith

pancreat/o/path/y
pan kre at op' a thi

706

Build a word meaning:
    excision of part or all of the pancreas

_____/_____

    incision into the pancreas

_____/_____

pancreat/ectomy
pan kre at ek' to mi

pancreatotomy
pan kre at ot' o mi

707

Now you may close your dictionary or anatomy book. Continue referring to page 84 for the next four frames.

a breather frame

708

Find hepat/o in your dictionary. Analyze four new words that involve the liver. Draw the diagonals.

hepatogenic
hepatoma
hepatomegaly
hepatopathy

I believe you!
You should be impressed with yourself.

709

When an entire gastrectomy is performed, a new connection (opening) is formed between the esophagus and duodenum. This is called an

_____/_____ _____/_____.

esophag/o/duoden/ostomy
esophagoduodenostomy
e sof a go du o den
    os' to me

91

Fun, wasn't it?

710

Analyze (make your own diagonal divisions):
gastroenterocolostomy

gastr o enter o col ostomy

esophagogastrostomy

esophag o gastr ostomy

enterocholecystostomy

enter o chol e cyst ostomy

711

Analyze (make your own diagonal divisions):
jejunoileostomy

jejun o ile ostomy

Amazing what can be done with a few odd word roots, isn't it?

duodenocholecystostomy

duoden o chol e cyst ostomy

esophagogastroscopy

esophag o gastr o scop y

712

Arteries (arteri/o) are vessels (angi/o) that carry blood from the heart. Veins are vessels which carry blood back to the _____.

heart

713

A word root–combining form for vein is phleb/o. Arteriosclerosis is hardening of the _____.
Hardening of veins is called
_____ / _____ / _____ / _____.

arteries
phleb/o/scler/osis
phlebosclerosis
fleb o skle ro' sis

714

Build a word meaning:
excision of a vein
_____ / _____

fixation of a vein
_____ / _____ / _____

phleb/ectomy
fleb ek' to mi

phleb/o/pex/y
fleb' o peks i

715

Build a word meaning:
venous dilatation (stretching)
_____ / _____

arterial dilatation
_____ / _____

vessel dilatation
_____ / _____

phlebectasia
fleb ek ta' zi a

arteriectasia
ar te ri ek ta' zi a

angiectasia
an ji ek ta' zi a

716

Phleb/o/plasty means

surgical repair of a vein

** _____

incision into a vein or
venisection

Phleb/otomy means

** _____

Work Review Sheets 12 and 13.

717

Another combining form that you can use as a suffix is **orrhexis**. orrhexis means rupture. Hyster/

rupture of the uterus

orrhexis means ** _____

_____ .

718

With orrhexis you learn the last of the "rrh" forms. Neither of the four is a real suffix. But since they have involved development, you are fortunate to

suffixes

be able to use them as _____ .

719

Cyst/orrhexis means

rupture of the bladder

** _____ .

rupture of the small
  intestine

Enter/orrhexis means

** _____ .

720

Build a word meaning:
  rupture of the heart

cardi/orrhexis
kar di or reks' is

_____/_____

angi/orrhexis
an ji or eks' is

  rupture of a vessel

_____/_____

721

Build a word meaning:
  rupture of an artery

arteri/orrhexis
ar te ri or eks' is

_____/_____

phleborrhexis
fleb or reks' is

  rupture of a vein

_____/_____

93

722

Build a word meaning:
  rupture of the liver

hepat/orrhexis

_____/_____

  suturing of the liver

hepat/orrhaphy

_____/_____

hepat/orrhea
(You pronounce)

  flowing from the liver

_____/_____

723

Build a word meaning:
  rupture of the bladder

cystorrhexis

_____/_____

  hemorrhage from the bladder

cystorrhagia

_____/_____

  flowing from the bladder

cystorrhea

_____/_____

cystorrhaphy
(You pronounce)

  suturing of the bladder

_____/_____

724

Esthesia is a word meaning feeling or sensation.
an is a form of the prefix **a. an** means

without

_____.

725

Esthesia means
            **

feeling or sensation

_____.

Analyze the following words:
  esthesiometer

esthesi/o/meter

_____/____/_____

  esthesioscopy

esthesi/o/scop/y

_____/___/_____/_____

  anesthesia

an/esthesi/a

_____/_____/_____

an/esthesi/o/log/y
(You pronounce)

  anesthesiology

___/_____/___/____/_____

94

726

Analyze the following words (you do the dividing):
anesthesiologist

an/esthesi/o/log/ist

_____

dysesthesia

dys/esthesi/a

hypo/esthesi/a
(You pronounce)

hypoesthesia

_____

727

Algesia is a word meaning overly sensitive to pain.
Hyper/esthesi/a is a synonym for algesia. Algesia

over sensitivity to pain or
hyperesthesia

means ** _____

_____.

728

Analyze the following words (remember to **think**
as you analyze):
algesimeter

alges/i/meter

_____ / ____ / _____

algesic (adjective)

alges/ic

_____ / _____

algesia (noun)

alges/ia

an/alges/ia
(You pronounce)

_____ / _____

analgesia

_____ / _____ / _____

729

Analyze the following words (you do the dividing):

an/alges/ia

analgesia _____

hyperalgesia

hyper/alges/ia

_____

paralgesia

par/alges/ia

par/algia
(You pronounce)

around area of pain

paralgia

_____

730

Par/**a** means beside, beyond, around or abnormal.

inflammation around the
kidney

Paranephritis means
** _____.

inflammation around the
liver

Parahepatitis means
** _____.

731

Analyze the following words:

paranephritis

_____/____/_____/_____

par/a/nephr/itis _kidney_ *paralysis*

paraplegia

_____/____/_____/_____

par/a/pleg/ia ⬅

paralysis

_____/____/_____/_____

par/a/lys/is
pa ral' i sis ⬅
(You pronounce)

732

Analyze the following words (you divide them):

parasalpingitis

_____

par/a/salping/itis

parahepatitis

_____

par/a/hepat/itis
par/a/oste/o/arthr/o/
  path/y
(You pronounce)

paraosteoarthropathy

_____

733

Analyze the following words (**phas/o** means speech):

abnormal speech

paraphasia

_____/____/_____/_____

par/a/phas/ia

aphasia

_____/_____/_____

a/phas/ia

tachyphasia

_____/____/_____/_____

tach/y/phas/ia

bradyphasia

_____/____/_____/_____

brad/y/phas/ia
(You pronounce)

734

Analyze the following words:

dysphasia

_____

dys/phas/ia

hyperphasia

_____

hyper/phas/ia

dysphonia _voice_

_____

dys/phon/ia

hypophonia

_____

hypo/phon/ia
(You pronounce)

96

735
Phas/o means speech.
Phon/o means voice.
Tachyphasia means
**

rapid speech

Dysphonia means
**

weak voice (poor etc.)

736
Bradyphasia means
**

slow speech

Aphonia means
**

without voice

Phonic means
**

pertaining to the voice
an instrument for
    measuring intensity
    of voice

A phonometer is
**

737
Analyze the following words:
    phonocardiography
    _____ / _____ / _____ / _____ / _____ / _____

phon/o/cardi/o/graph/y
Sound heart chart

    phonomyography
    _____ / _____ / _____ / _____ / _____ / _____

phon/o/my/o/graph/y

    phonomyogram
    _____ / _____ / _____ / _____ / _____

phon/o/my/o/gram
voice - study of
phon/o/log/y
(You pronounce)

    phonology
    _____ / _____ / _____ / _____

738
Look up my/o in your dictionary. How many columns of words begin with my/o? _____ My/o
is used in words referring to

5 to 8

muscle(s)

_____.

739
Analyze the first four words from the dictionary
beginning with my/o, whose parts you have already
learned:

my/o/a/troph/y
my/o/blast
my/o/blast/oma
my/o/brad/ia
my/o/cardi/a
my/o/card/itis

without muscle development
muscle
m

(Your answers will vary with the dictionary used.
Pick the proper four in the answer column.)

740

Go to my/o/fasc/itis in the dictionary. Analyze the next four words whose parts you already know:

my/o/fibr/il
my/o/fibr/oma
my/o/fibr/osis
my/o/fibr/o/sitis
my/o/gen/esis
my/o/gen/ic

_____

_____

_____

_____

(Your answers will vary with the dictionary used. Pick the proper four in the answer column.)

741

Using the words myogram through myography in the dictionary, fill these blanks:

myogram _____ / ___ / _____ the chart

myograph _____ / ___ / _____ the instrument

myography
(You pronounce) _____ / ___ / _____ / ___ the description (also the process)

my/o/hemat/in *hormone*
my/o/hyster/ectomy
my/oid
my/o/kinesi/meter
my/o/kinesi/s
my/o/lip/oma

742

Analyze the next five word parts you recognize:

_____

_____

_____

_____

_____

(Your answer will vary with the dictionary used. Pick the proper five in the answer column.)

743

For your own interest, count how many words you know beginning with my/o. Write the number here.

over 60

_____ .

744

muscles

When you see my/o, you will think of _____ .
(I don't mean eight columns of words!)

Work Review Sheets 14 and 15.

745

Dipl/o means double. Dipl/o/cardi/a means having

heart
double
double

a double _____ . Dipl/o/genesis means producing _____ parts or _____ substances.

98

746

Dipl/o/blast/ic means having two germ (embryonic) layers. Form a word meaning having two **voice** tones (at the same time).

_____ / _____ / _____ / ia .

747

opia is an involved form that we can use as a suffix. **opia** means vision. Build a word meaning

double vision. _____ / _____ .

748

~~These~~ *there* are many kinds of diplopia. "Crossed eyes"

cause one kind of _____ / _____ .

749

Whenever both eyes fail to record the same image on the brain, _____ occurs.

750

Amb/i means both or both sides. Amb/i/later/al means pertaining to _____ sides.

751

An amb/i/dextr/ous person can work well with _____ hands.

752

A word that means separate **vision** with both eyes

is _____ / _____ / _____ .

753

The result of separate vision from both eyes is a double image or double vision. Medically, double vision can be expressed either as

_____ / _____ or

_____ / _____ / _____ .

754

You cannot work this frame unless you are using Taber's dictionary. However, you must know the word meanings from another dictionary. Look up ambivalence in your dictionary. Read what it means. Analyze it and the following two words here:

_____ / _____ / _____ / _____

_____ / _____ / _____ / _____

_____ / _____ / _____ / _____

dipl/o/phon/ia
diplophonia
dip lo fo' ni a

dipl/opia
diplopia
dip lo' pi a

diplopia

diplopia

both

both

amb/i/opia
ambiopia
am be o' pi a

dipl/opia

ambiopia

amb/i/valen/ce
am biv' a lens
amb/i/valen/cy
am biv' a lens e
amb/i/valen/t
am biv' a lent

755

A dipl/o/bacteri/um is a bacterium that occurs in pairs or doubly. A coccus that grows in pairs is a ___/___/___/___.

dipl/o/cocc/us
diplococcus
dip lo kok' us

756

Hyperopia means farsightedness (vision). A word that means blue vision is ___/___.

cyanopia
si an op' i a

757

Neur/o is used in words that refer to nerves. Neur/algia means pain along the course of a ___.

nerve

758

Neuroarthropathy is a disease of _____ and _____.

nerves
joints

759

Neurology is the medical speciality that deals with the nervous system. A man who specializes in diseases of the nervous system is a ___/___/___.

neur/o/log/ist
neurologist
nu rol' o jist

760

Build a word meaning:

inflammation of a nerve

___/___

destruction of nerve tissue

___/___/___

surgical repair of nerves

___/___/___/___

neuritis
nu ri' tis

neurolysis
nu rol' is is

neuroplasty
nu' ro plas ti

761

Neur/o/trips/y means surgical crushing of a nerve. The word root for crushing (usually by rubbing or grinding) is _____.

trips

762

Trips/is, from which we get **trips/y,** is a Greek word that means "rub" or "massage." Tripsis can be carried to the point of crushing or grinding. Surgical crushing of a nerve is ___/___/___/___.

neur/o/trips/y
nu' ro trip si

100

763

In some cases of lithiasis, it may be necessary to crush calculi so they may be passed. A word to mean surgical crushing of stones is

lithotripsy

_____ / _____ / _____ .

double meaning

764

Look up myel/itis in your dictionary (dictionary work through Frame 766). From the definition, you conclude that **myel** is the word root for

spinal cord
bone marrow

*_____ and

*_____ .

765

Find the word myeloblast. Analyze it:

myel/o/blast
mi' el o blast

_____ / _____ / _____ . The combin-

myel/o

ing form of myel is _____ / _____ .

766

Find a word meaning:

pertaining to myelocytes

myel/o/cyt/ic
mi el o sit' ik

_____ / _____ / _____ / _____

herniation of the spinal cord

myel/o/cele
mi' el o sel

_____ / _____ / _____

defective (poor or bad) formation of the spinal cord

myel/o/dys/plas/ia
mi el o dis pla' zi a

_____ / _____ / dys / plas / ia

767

Plas/ia, plas/is means formation or change in the sense of molding. This kind of formation occurs naturally instead of being done by a plastic surgeon. Dys/plas/ia means **_____

defective (poor or abnor-
mal) formation

_____ .

768

A/plas/ia means failure of an organ to develop properly. A word that means overgrowth or too much development is

hyper/plas/ia
hyperplasia
hi per pla' zi a

_____ / _____ .

769

If overdevelopment is hyperplasia, underdevelopment is expressed as

hypoplasia
hi po pla zi a

_____ / _____ .

101

770

Using myel/o/dys/plas/ia as a model, build a word meaning:

defective development of cartilage

chondr/o/dys/plas/ia /is

_____/____/_____/____/_____

defective formation of bone and cartilage

oste/o/chondr/o/dys/ plas/ia /is

_____/____/_____/___/____/_____

771

Form a word meaning inflammation of nerves and spinal cord:

neur/o/myel/itis
neuromyelitis
nu ro mi el i' tis

_____/____/_____/_____

772

free frame

Psych/o comes from the Greek "psyche." Both words mean soul or mind. In a Webster's Collegiate Dictionary, look up psycho and Psyche. Read the definitions. Look at how many words in everyday English begin with the word root psych.

773

from 5 to 9
(depending on
dictionary used)

Turn in your medical dictionary to words beginning with psych. **Psych** words occupy approximately _____ (how many) columns.

774

M.O.

Psychiatry is the field of medicine that studies and deals with mental and neurotic disorders. The physician who specializes in this field of medicine is called a

psychiatrist
si ki' a trist

_____.

775

P. M. D.
consuleng

Psych/o/log/y is the science that studies the mind and mental process. The scientist who works in this field is called a

psych/o/log/ist
psychologist
si kol' o gist

_____/___/_____/_____.

(Psychiatry is the medical branch of psychology.)

776

psych/osis
psychosis
si ko' sis

Psych/o/genesis means the formation of mental traits. A word that means any abnormal mental **condition** is _____/_____.

102

777

A psych/o/neur/osis is a disease that is mainly mental in origin. A psych/o/neur/o/tic person is one who suffers from a

_____ / / _____ / _____ .

psych/o/neur/osis
si ko nu ro' sis

778

The patient suffering from a psychoneurosis knows the real from the unreal. He only exaggerates the reality. The person who is blinded on a normally bright day **may** suffer from a

_____ .

psychoneurosis

779

Psychoneuroses (plural) take many forms. Hysteria, psych/asthenia, and neur/asthenia are forms of

_____ / / _____ / _____ .

psychoneuroses

780

In your medical dictionary read about the **psychopath** and the **psychopathic** personality. Also read the definition of **psychopathy.** In Frame 781 analyze these three words.

free frame

soul or mind

781

_____

_____

_____

psych/o/<u>path</u> disease
psych/o/path/ic adj.
psych/o/path/y noun.
si kop' ath i

782

Let your eye wander down the columns of "psych" words. Read about any that interest you. Did you read the section following the words psychiatric and psychoanalysis? All psych/o words refer to

_____ .

mind or soul

783

In Webster's dictionary look at the words beginning with gnos. They come from the Greek word meaning _____ .

knowledge

784

In your medical dictionary find the word **gnosia** or **gnosis.** It, too, is built from the Greek word meaning _____ .

knowledge

103

785

In your dictionary, you may have noticed when you were reading the discussion of many diseases a section headed **prog.** This stands for pro/gnos/is which means foreknowledge or predicting the outcome of a disease. The prefix that means "before or in front of" is _____ .

pro *before*

786

If you look at leukemia, acute, in Taber's dictionary, you will find that the pro/gnosis is fatal within three months. For leukemia, myelogenous, the

_____/_____ is fatal in three to four years.

prognosis
prog no' sis

787

Procephalic means **in the front** of the head. Analyze procephalic.

_____/_____/_____

Prognostic means giving an indication to the outcome of a disease. Analyze prognostic.

_____/_____/

pro/cephal/ic
pro se fal' ik

pro/gnos/tic
prog nos' tik

788

Di/a means through. Di/ag/nos/is literally means
** _____ .

knowing through
or know through

789

A di/a/gnos/is of a disease is made by studying **through** its symptoms. When a patient tells a physician that he has chills, hot spells, and a runny nose, the physician may make a

_____/____/_____/_____ of a head cold.

di/a/gnos/is
diagnosis
di ag no' sis

790

Symptoms may become very complex. It may be necessary to do much laboratory work. When all this information is in the hands of a skilled diagnostician, a _____ may be made.

diagnosis

791

Build a word meaning without comprehension (knowledge):

_____/_____/ ia .

a/gnos/ia
ag no' si a

104

792

flowing through

The literal meaning of di/a/rrhea is **_____

_____ .

793

Di/a/therm/y means generating heat through (tissues).

through   Di/a means _____ .

heat   Therm means _____ .

suffix or ending   **y** is a noun _____ .

794

Therm/o is the word root–combining form which means heat. An instrument to measure heat is a

therm/o/meter
ther mom' e ter

            /   /
_____ .

795

Build a word meaning:

therm/al or therm/ic

  pertaining to heat _____ / _____

therm/o/esthesia or
therm/o/algesia

  oversensitivity to heat

               /   /
_____

therm/o/genesis
(You pronounce)

  formation of body heat

  orgen   /   /
_____

796

Build a word meaning:

  abnormal fear of heat

therm/o/phob/ia

         /   /   /
_____

  heatstroke (paralysis)

therm/o/pleg/ia

         /   /   /
_____

di/a/therm/y
(You pronounce)

  heating through tissue

         /   /   /
_____

797

If you ever want information about temperature scales or variations of body temperature, you would look in the dictionary for words beginning with

therm or therm/o
(Try it!)

_____ .

Work Review Sheets 16 and 17.

798

A micr/o/scop/e is an instrument for examining something small. An instrument for examining "through" is a

di/a/scop/e
di' as kop

         /   /   /
_____ .

105

799

A diascope is placed on the skin, and the skin is looked "through" to see changes. The word part

di/a

for **through** is _____/_____.

800

Micr/o/ means small. Hydr/o/cephal/us is a condition involving fluid in the head. An abnormally small head is

micr/o/cephal/us
mik ro sef' a lus

_____/_____/_____/_____.

801

Microcephalus limits the size of the brain. Most microcephalic people are mentally retarded. Occasionally a baby is born with an unusually small head or

micr/o/cephal/us

_____/_____/_____/_____.

802

A cyst is a sac containing fluid. You also use cyst/o in building words pertaining to cysts.

A very small cyst is a

micr/o/cyst
mi' kro sist

_____/_____/_____.

A very small cell is a

micr/o/cyt/e
mi' kro sit

_____/_____/_____.

A small heart is

micr/o/cardi/a
mi kro kar' di a

_____/_____/_____.

803

An instrument for measuring something microscopic is a

micr/o/meter
mi krom' e ter

_____/_____/_____. The micron (1/1000 mm) is the unit of measurement. Many cocci are 2 microns in diameter. A red blood

micron(s)
mi' kron

cell is 7 _____ in diameter.

804

Macr/o is the opposite of micr/o. Macr/o is used

large

in words to mean _____.

805

Things that are macr/o/scop/ic can be seen with the naked eye. Very large cells are called

macr/o/cyt/e(s)
mak' ro sit

_____/_____/_____.

806

An abnormally large head is

_____/____/_____/_____ .

A large embryonic (germ) cell is a

_____/____/_____ .

A very large coccus is called a

_____/____/_____/_____ .

macrocephalus

macroblast

macrococcus
(You pronounce)

807

Macr/o/gloss/ia means ** _____ .
Macr/ot/ia means ** _____ .
Macr/o/rhin/ia means ** _____ .
Macr/o/cheil/ia means ** _____ .

abnormally:
  large tongue
  large ear(s)
  large nose
  large lips

808

Macr/o/dactyl/ia means abnormally large fingers or toes. The word root for fingers or toes is

_____ .

dactyl

809

Another way of saying large fingers or toes is dactyl/o/megal/y. The combining form for finger or toe is _____/_____ .

dactyl/o

810

A finger or toe is called a digit. (When you see digit, finger, or toe, use dactyl/o.) Build a word meaning:

  inflammation of a digit

_____/_____

  cramp or spasm of a digit

_____/____/_____

  a fingerprint

_____/____/____ gram

dactyl/itis
dak til i' tis

dactyl/o/spasm
dak' til o spazm

dactyl/o/gram
dak til o gram

811

Macr/o/dactyl/ia means
  ** _____ .

Poly/dactyl/ism means too many
    ** _____ .

abnormally large
fingers and toes
(digits)
fingers or toes
(digits)

812

Pol/y is a combining form that means too many or too much. Pol/y/ur/ia means excessive amount of urine. When a person drinks too much water,

pol/y/ur/ia
pol i u' ri a

_____ / / _____ / _____ results.

813

Pol/y/neur/o/path/y means disease of many nerves. The word for inflammation of many nerves

pol/y/neur/itis
polyneuritis
pol i nu ri' tis

is _____ / / _____ / _____ .

814

Build a word meaning:
  inflammation of many joints

pol/y/arthr/itis
pol i ar thri' tis

_____ / / _____ / _____

  pain in several nerves

pol/y/neur/algia
pol i nu ral' ji a

_____ / / _____ / _____

  having more than two ears

pol/y/ot/ia
pol i o' shi a

_____ / / _____ / _____

815

many cysts

Pol/y/cyst/ic means ** _____ .

eating too much

Pol/y/phag/ia means ** _____ .

excessive fear of things
(too many phobias)

Pol/y/phob/ia means ** _____ .

816

Syn/dactyl/ism means a joining of two or more digits. The prefix that means together or joined is

syn _sin_

_____ .

817

Syn/ergetic means working together. Drugs that work together to increase each other's effects are

syn/ergetic
synergetic
sin er jet' ik

called _____ / _____ drugs.

818

Synergetic muscles are muscles that work together. There are three muscles that work together to flex

synergetic

the forearm. They are _____ muscles.

819

APC tablets are more effective for killing pain than aspirin alone. This is because aspirin, phenacetin,

synergetic

and caffine are _____

drugs.

108

820

Analyze synarthrosis:

syn

arthr

osis

    prefix   _____

    word root (joint)   _____

    condition   _____

821

A syn/arthr/osis is an immovable joint. The joining bones are fused together. When bones are fused at a joint so that there is no movement, the joint is a

syn/arthr/osis
synarthrosis
sin ar thro' sis

_____ / _____ / _____ .

822

information frame

pro drom
syn drom

Drom/o comes from the Greek word for "run." A drom/o/mania is an insane impulse to wander or roam. You usually use **drom** with the prefixes syn and pro. In this usage, it is a symptom that is "running."

823

A syn/drome is a variety of symptoms occurring (meaning running along) together. The complete picture of a disease is its

syndrome
sin' drom

_____ .

824

Look up syndrome in your dictionary. Read about Korsakoff's syndrome. Note some others. A syndrome due to alcoholism is

Korsakoff's syndrome

_____

_____ .

825

Pro/drome means running before (a disease). Symptoms that indicate an approaching disease

pro/drome
prodrome
pro' drom

are its _____ / _____ .

826

The sneezes that come before a common cold are

prodrome

the _____ of the cold.

827

Pro/drom/al is the adjectival form of pro/drom/e. A rash that shows before the true macules of mea-

pro/drom/al
prodromal
prod' ro mal

sles is called a _____ / _____ / _____

rash.

828

Chickenpox also has a

prodromal

_____ rash.

829

Pol/y/dips/ia means excessive thirst (desire for **too much** fluid). The word root for thirst is

dips

_____.

830

Pol/y/dips/ia can be caused by something as simple as eating too much salt. A highly salted meal may cause

pol/y/dips/ia
polydipsia
pol i dip' si a

_____ / _____ / _____ / _____.

831

Polydipsia can be caused by something as complex as an upset in pituitary secretion. If the pituitary gland secretes too much of one hormone, salt is retained in the body, and

polydipsia

_____ results.

832

Large doses of some forms of cortisone also cause

polydipsia

_____.

833

Dips/o/mania is a way of saying alcoholism. A person who drinks excessively of alcoholic beverages suffers from

dips/o/mania
dipsomania
dip so ma' ni a

_____ / _____ / _____.

834

A dips/o/mani/ac is a person who suffers from dips/o/mania. A person with Korsakoff's syndrome is usually a

dips/o/mani/ac
dipsomaniac
dip so ma' ni ak

_____ / _____ / _____ / _____.

835

Build a word meaning:
  condition of thirst

dips/osis
dipsosis
dip so' sis

_____ / _____

  treatment by (limiting) water intake

dips/o/therap/y
dip so ther' a pi

_____ / _____ / _____ / _____

Work Review Sheets 18 and 19.

Use this picture to help work the next page.

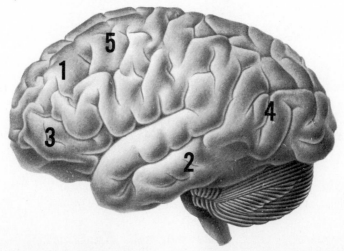

In the biological sciences there are many directional words. This page is to help you understand the use of six of them. Label the drawings on the basis of the information given. Use this page while working frames 848 through 853.

DIRECTIONAL WORD	COMBINING FORM	MEANING
dorsal	dors/al–dors/o (back)	near or on the back
ventral	ventr/al–ventr/o (belly)	near or on the belly side of the body
anterior	anter/ior–anter/o (before)	toward the front or in front of
posterior	poster/ior–poster/o (behind after)	following or located behind
cephalic	cephal/ic–cephal/o (head)	upward–toward the head
caudal caudad	caud/al–caud/o /ad (tail)	downward–toward the tail

Dog

836 *dorsal*

837 *chepalic* 841 *posterior*

838 *anterior* 840 *caudad*

839 *ventral*

Man

842 *cephalic*

843 *ventral* 847 *dorsal*

844 *anterior* 846 *posterior*

845 *caudal*

Check your answers with the correct labels at the bottom of the next page.

Analyze the words in the next six frames (you draw the lines)

848

anter/o/later/al	anterolateral (side)	*in front & too one side*
anter/o/medi/an	anteromedian (middle)	*in front & toward center line*
anter/o/super/io (You pronounce)	anterosuperior (above)	*in front & above*

849

poster/o/later/al	posterolateral (side)	*in behind too one side*
poster/o/extern/al	posteroexternal (outer)	*toward back & outer side*
poster/o/intern/al (You pronounce)	posterointernal (inner)	*toward back & inter side*

850

anter/o/poster/ior	anteroposterior	*passing from front to rear*
dors/o/cephal/ad	dorsocephalad	*toward back of head*
dors/o/dynia (You pronounce)	dorsodynia	*back pain in upper part*

851

ventr/ad	ventrad	*toward belly*
ventr/otomy	ventrotomy	*incision into belly*
ventr/o/scop/y e (You pronounce)	ventroscope	*instrument to examine belly area*

Dog

dorsal

change
anterior   posterior

cephalic   caudad
               al

ventral

Man

cephalic

ventral   dorsal

anterior   posterior

caudad
   al

112

852

cephal/ad

cephal/o/trips/y

cephal/o/meter

cephalad _toward the head_

cephalotripsy _crushing of head (procedure_

cephalometer ~~measuring of the head~~

instrument to measure the head

853

caud/a

caud/ate

caud/ation

(You pronounce)

cauda _tail_

caudate _possessing the tail_

caudation _having a tail_

854

Aer/o is used in words to mean air. You undoubtedly know the words aer/ial, and aer/ialist. You probably use an aer/o/sol bomb to kill insects. Aer/o always makes you think of _____.

air

855

Using what you need of aer/o, build a word meaning:

abnormal fear of air

_____ / _____ / _____ / _____

aer/o/phob/ia

a er o fo' bi a

treatment with air

_____ / _____ / _____ / _____

aer/o/therap/y

herniation containing air

_____ / _____

aer/o/cele

(You pronounce)

856

Bios is the Greek word for life. Bi/o/chemistry is the study of chemical changes in living things. The science (study of) living things is

_____ / _____ / _____ / _____ .

bi/o/log/y

857

A biologist is one who studies

living things or life

** ** ʼ

_____ .

Biogenesis is the formation of _again_

living things

** **

_____ .

858

An an/aer/o/bi/c plant or animal cannot live in the presence of air (**an**—without). Analyze anaerobic:

an

prefix (without)   _____

aer/o

combining form (air) _____ / _____

bi

word root (life)   _____

c

adjectival ending   _____

859

If anaerobic means existing without air (oxygen), build a word that means needing air (oxygen) to live (adjectival form):

aer/o/bi/c
aerobic
a er o' bik

_____ / _____ / _____ .

860

Use aerobic or anaerobic in the following sentences (four frames).
The bacterium that causes pneumonia requires air to live. These bacteria are considered

aerobic

_____ bacteria.

861

The tetanus bacillus causes lockjaw. Lockjaw can only develop in closed wounds where air does not penetrate (e.g., stepping on an old nail). The tetanus bacillus is an _____ bacterium.

anaerobic
an er o' bik

862

Botulism is a serious type of food poisoning. It occurs from eating improperly canned meats and vegetables. Cans do not admit air. The bacillus that causes botulism is _____ .

anaerobic

863

When a physician opens a wound so the air can reach it, he is protecting against infection by an _____ bacterium.

anaerobic

864

A **bi**/o/psy is an examination of _____ tissue.

living or live

865

A combining form that means color is chrom/o. The Greek word for a color is "chroma." There are English words chroma and chrome. Chrom/o makes you think of _____ .

color

866

A chromocyte is any colored cell. An **embryonic** color (pigment) cell is called a

chrom/o/blast
chromoblast
kro' mo blast

_____ / _____ / _____ .

867

Build a word meaning:
 destruction of color (in a cell)

_/ / /_

~~green~~
~~formation~~ of pigment (color)

_/ / /_

instrument for measuring amount of color in a substance

_/ /_

868

A chrom/o/phil/ic cell is one that takes a stain easily. Some leukocytes stain deeper than others. They are more

_/ / /_ than

the less easily stained leukocytes.

869

Some cells will not stain at all. They are not

_._

870

Some cells stain with one dye but not with another. They are differentially

_._

871

Chromophilic means
** _._ The
word that means something does not (without) stain easily is

_/ / /_ .

872

dys means * _._
The opposite of **dys** is **eu. eu** means
** _._

873

Form the word that means the opposite of:

dys/peps/ia _/ /_

dys/pept/ic _/ /_

dys/pne/a _/ /_

115

chrom/o/lys/is
kro mol' is is

chrom/o/genes/is
kro mo jen' e sis

chrom/o/meter
kro mom' e ter

chrom/o/phil/ic
chromophilic
kro mo fil' ik

chromophilic

chromophilic

staining easily
a/chrom/o/phil/ic

achromophilic
a kro' mo fil ik

bad, painful, or
difficult

well or easy
eu pronounced you

eu/peps/ia
u pep' si a
eu/pept/ic
u pep' tic
eu/pne/a
up ne' a

874

Form the opposite of:

dys/kinesi/a

_____/_____/

eu/kinesi/a
u kin e' si a

dys/esthesi/a

_____/_____/

eu/esthesi/a
u es the' si a

dys/phor/ia

_____/_____/

eu/phor/ia
u fo' ri a

875

easy or normal labor
and childbirth

Dys/tocia means difficult labor. Eutocia means
_____.

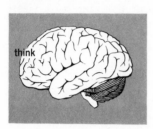

think

876

This course is meant to teach you medical terminology—not to learn it for you. If you work a frame
and have forgotten what the word root means,
look it up.

877

direction frame
for 878

(Frames 878–880 are best worked with Taber's
dictionary only.) Turn to the forgotten (or new)
word in your medical dictionary. Following the pronunciation is a bracketed [ ] section giving the
origin of the word. If the [ ] reads [+ G.–itis], go
to the first word in the dictionary starting with this
word root to find the meaning of the root.

878

Use the dictionary to find the meaning of the word
roots in the following:

treatment
movement
kidney

therapeutic   _____

kinesia   _____

nephrectomy   _____

879

If you want a word root and have forgotten it, look
up the word for which you want a root. You should
not have to read far until you recognize the root
you want.

880

Use the dictionary to find the word root for:

cephal

py

head   _____

pus   _____

881

Men/o is used in words referring to the menses.
Men/ses is another way of saying men/struation.
Men/o in any word should make you think of

menses or menstruation

_____ .

882

Men/o/pause means permanent cessation of

menstruation or menses

_____ .

excessive menstruation
or menstrual hemorrhage

Men/orrhagia means
    **
_____ .

883

Men/o/phania refers to a girl's first menstrual
period. Build a word meaning:
    flow of menses

men/orrhea
men or e' a

             /
_____

dys/men/orrhea
dis men or e' a

    painful (bad or difficult) menstrual flow
        /   /
_____

884

Build a word meaning:
    absence (without) menstrual flow

a/men/orrhea
a men o re' a

       /   /
_____

men/o/stasis
men os' ta sis

    *suppression of menstrual flow
         /   /
_____

885

Hem/o/stasis[1] means
     **
_____ .

controlling blood flow
phleb/o/stasis
fleb os' ta sis
(also venostasis)

A word meaning control of flow in veins is
       /   /
_____ .

886

Build a word meaning:
    control of flow in arteries

arteri/o/stasis
ar ter i os' ta sis

       /   /
_____

lymph/o/stasis
limf os' ta sis

    control of lymph flow
       /   /
_____

[1]Stasis is a word meaning stopping or controlling.

117

887

Syphilis is a venereal disease. Read about the disease in your dictionary. Note the origin of the word. Look at the words beginning with **syphil.** The combining form used in words referring to this disease is _____ / _____ .

syphil/o

888

Analyze the last four words in your dictionary that begin with syphil.

syphilonthus

Syphilous

syphilotheraphy

syphilosis

syphil/o/psych/osis
syphil/osis
syphil/ous
syphil/o/phobe
syphil/o/phob/ia
syphil/o/phyma
syphil/o/tropic
syphil/o/therap/y

(The answers will vary with the dictionary used. Pick the proper four in the answer column.)

889

Build a word meaning:
  a syphilitic tumor

_____ / _____

syphiloma

  resembling syphilis

_____ / _____

syphiloid

  any syphilitic disease

_____ / _____ / _____

syphilopathy
(You pronounce)

suido

890

Pseud/o means false. A pseudocyesis is a false pregnancy. A pseudoscience is a

*_____ .

false science

891

Pseud/o/mania is a psychosis in which the patient falsely accuses himself of crimes. Pseud/o/paral-ysis means ** _____

_____ .

false paralysis
(paralysis not due
to nerve damage)

892

Build a word meaning:
  a false cyst

_____ / _____ / _____

pseud/o/cyst
su' do sist

  false edema

_____ / _____ / _____

pseud/o/edema
su do e de' ma

  false sensation

_____ / _____ / _____

pseud/o/esthesi/a
su do es the' zi a

Look up and learn the meaning of **edema.**

*edema -
Swelling of fluid
such as swelling of ankles*

893

Build a word meaning:
false hypertrophy

pseud/o/hyper/troph/y   _____ / ____ / _____ / _____ / _____

false tuberculosis

pseud/o/tubercul/osis   _____ / ____ / _____ / _____

pseud/o/syphil/is   false syphilis
(You pronounce)   _____ / ____ / _____ / _____

894

The viscera are the internal organs of the body. Viscerad means toward the viscera. Viscerogenic is also a word. The word root–combining form for

viscer/o   viscera is _____ / _____ .

895

In the words viscer/o/motor, viscer/o/pariet/al,

organs   and viscer/o/pleur/al, viscer/o refers to
(internal organs)

_____ .

896

Build a word meaning:
prolapse of organs

viscer/o/ptosis
vis er op to' sis   _____ / ____ / _____

viscer/algia   pain in organs
vis er al' ji a

_____ / _____

viscer/al   pertaining to organs
vis' ser al

_____ / _____

897

Analyze:
viscerosensory

viscer/o/sens/ory   _____

visceroskeletal

viscer/o/skelet/al   _____

wat

viscer/o/gen/ic   viscerogenic

_____

Work Review Sheets 20 and 21.

898

Lapar/o means abdominal wall. A laparectomy is
an excision of part of the

abdominal wall   * _____ .

899

lapar/otomy
lap ar ot' o mi

An incision into the abdominal wall is a

_____ / _____ .

lapar/orrhaphy
lap ar or' ra fi

A suturing of the abdominal wall is

_____ / _____ .

900

Analyze the following words:

lapar/o/hepat/otomy

   laparohepatotomy _____

lapar/o/col/ostomy

   laparocolostomy _____

lapar/o/gastr/otomy

   laparogastrotomy _____

901

There may be longer words than this. If there are, there are not many. Analyze it for fun. Think of the word parts.

You couldn't be wrong

Laparohysterosalpingo-oophorectomy _____

_____

902

Pyr/o is used in words to mean heat or fever. (Remember the funeral pyres on which the Greeks and Romans burned their dead?) A pyromaniac is one who has a madness for starting or seeing

fires

_____ .

903

pyr/osis
pyrosis
pi ro' sis

Pyr/exia means fever. A condition of heat (heartburn) is _____ / _____ .

904

Build a word meaning:

   instrument for measuring heat

pyr/o/meter

_____ / _____

   destruction by fever

pyr/o/lysis

_____ / _____

   abnormal fear of fire

pyr/o/phob/ia
Can you pronounce these?

_____ / _____ / _____

905

fever or
high body
temperature etc.

A pyr/o/toxin is a toxin (poison) produced by

_____ ** _____ .

120

Use this information for building words involving color
(Frames 906 through 910)

earth

leuk/o	white
melan/o	black
erythr/o	red
cyan/o	blue
chlor/o	green
xanth/o	yellow

zantho

906
Cyan/opia means blue vision. Form a word mean-ing:

xanth/opia
zan thop' i a
chlor/opia
klo ro' pi a
erythr/opia
er i throp' i a

yellow vision _____/_____

green vision _____/_____

red vision

_____/_____

907
Cyan/o/derma means blue skin. Build a word meaning:
red skin (blushing)

erythr/o/derma

_____/___/_____

white skin

leuk/o/derma

_____/___/_____

yellow skin

xanth/o/derma

_____
(You draw the lines)

melan/o/derma
(You pronounce)

black (discolored) skin

_____

908
Build a word meaning:
green cell (plants only)

chlor/o/cyte

_____/___/_____

black cell (dark)

melan/o/cyte

_____/___/_____

white (blood) cell

leuk/o/cyte

_____/___/_____

red (blood) cell

erythr/o/cyte
(You pronounce)

_____/___/_____

121

909

Build a word meaning an embryonic cell of the following color:

leuk/o/blast	white	___/___/___
melan/o/blast	black	___/___/___
chlor/o/blast	green	___/___/___
erythr/o/blast		
(You pronounce)	red	___/___/___

910

Cyan/emia is blue blood. (Not literally in people; lobsters have blue blood.) Build words involving the following colors in blood:

xanth/emia	yellow	_____/_____
chlor/emia	green	_____/_____
erythr/emia		
(You pronounce)	red (blushing)	_____/_____

911

green	Chlor/o	means _____.
yellow	Xanth/o	means _____.
red	Erythr/o	means _____.
white	Leuk/o	means _____.
black	Melan/o	means _____.

912

Hydr/o means water or fluid. Hidr/o means sweat. A hidr/o/cyst/oma is a cystic tumor of a

sweat

_____ gland.

913

inflammation of sweat glands

Hidr/o/aden/itis means ** _____

_____.

914

There are three words that mean excessive sweating. Analyze them:

hidrosis

hidr/osis

_____

hyperhidrosis

hyper/hidr/osis

_____

~~hidr/orrhea~~ – *Suffix*
(You pronounce)
not word

hidrorrhea

_____

915

without sweat or absence of sweat

The word an/hidr/osis means ** _____

_____.

916

Both **hydr/o** and **hidr/o** are pronounced alike.

water or fluid

Hydro with a "**y**" means _____.

sweat

Hidro with an "**i**" means _____.

917

Gynec/o comes from the Greek word "gyne" which means woman. The field of medicine called gyne-

women

cology deals with diseases of _____.

918

gynec/o/log/ist
gynecologist
jin e kol' o jist

g

Gynec/o/log/ic or gynec/o/log/ical are adjectival forms of gynecology. The physician who specializes in female disorders is called a

_____ / _____ / _____ / _____.

919

gynecoid
jin' e koid

g

gynecopathy

g ji ne kop' a thi

gynecophobia

g jin e ko fo' bi a

Build a word meaning:
resembling woman

_____ / _____

any disease peculiar to women

_____ / _____ / _____

abnormal fear of women

_____ / _____ / _____

920

Ophthalm/o is used in words to mean eye. Oph-
thalm/itis means

inflammation of the eye

_____*_____.

pertaining to the eye

Ophthalm/ic means

_____*_____.

921

Ophthalm/algia and ophthalm/o/dyn/ia both mean

pain in the eye

_____*_____.

922

practice pronouncing
look at the ph th

Before building words with this root, be sure you have the **phth** order of o**phth**alm/o straight. Pronounce it **off thalm o.**

923

ophthalm/o/cele
ophthalmocele
of thal' mo sel
ophthalm/o/meter
ophthalmometer
of thal mom' et er

Build a word meaning:
herniation of an eye (abnormal protrusion)

_____ / _____ / _____

instrument for measuring the eye

_____ / _____ / _____

123

924

Build a word meaning: ·
any eye disease

ophthalmopathy

_____ / /   /_____

plastic surgery of eye

ophthalmoplasty

_____ / /   /_____

ophthalmoplegia
(You pronounce)

paralysis of the eye

_____ / /   /_____

925

Ophthalmology is the medical speciality dealing with eye disease. We call the physician who practices this speciality an

ophthalmologist

_____ / /   /_____ .

926

Ophthalm/o/scop/y is the examination of the interior of the eye. The instrument used for this examination is an

ophthalmoscope

_____ / /   /_____ .

Fill in the chart on the next page. Check your answers on the following page. You will be formally introduced to some of the specialities in the field of medicine.

SPECIALITY	SPECIALIST	LIMITS OF FIELD
pathology	927	diseases—nature and causes
928	dermatologist	929
neurology	930	nervous conditions and diseases
931	gynecologist	female diseases
urology	932	male diseases
933	end/o/crin/o/log/ist	glands of internal secretion
oncology	934	neoplasms (new growths)
935	936	heart
ophthalmology	937	eye
938	otorhinolaryngologist	939 *ear nose Throat*

obstetrics	940	pregnancy, childbirth and puerperium
941	geriatrician	old age
pediatrics	942	children

orthopedics	orthopedist	bones and muscles
psychiatry	943	mental disorders

Check your answers on the next page.

SPECIALITY	SPECIALIST	LIMITS OF FIELD
	pathologist	
dermatology		skin
	neurologist	
gynecology		
	urologist	
endocrinology		
	oncologist	
cardiology	cardiologist	
	ophthalmologist	
otorhinolaryngology		ear–nose–throat

	obstetrician	
geriatrics		
	pediatrician	

	psychiatrist	

944

Glyc/o comes from the Greek word for "sweet."
Glyc/o/gen is "animal starch" formed from simple
sugars. The cells of the body use a simple sugar,
glucose, to release energy. To use its reserve fuel
supply of animal starch, the body must convert

_____ / / _____ to glucose.

glyc/o/gen
glycogen
gli' ko jen

945

Glucose is used by the muscles to release energy.
Glycogen is the reserve food supply of glucose.
Glucose is the usable form of

_____.

glycogen

946

Glycogen is potential sugar. Glucose is usable sugar.
In words, glyc/o should make you think of

_____.

sugar or sweet

947

Glyc/emia means sugar in the blood. Hyper/glyc/
emia means
** _____.

too much sugar in the
blood (high blood sugar)

948

Hyper/glyc/emia means high blood sugar. The
word that means low blood sugar is

_____.

hypoglycemia
hi po gli se' mi a

949 *argen*

The formation of glycogen from food is

_____ / / genesis _____.

glyc/o
glycogenesis
gli ko jen' es is

950

The breakdown (destruction) of sugar is
_____ / / / _____. The

discharge (flow) of sugar from the body is
_____ / _____.

glycolysis
gli kol' i sis

glycorrhea
gli kor re' a

951

Glyc/o/lip/id should make you think of two foods:
_____ and _____.

sugar
fat

952

The testicles are the organs in which the male germ
cells are formed. Spermatozoa are formed in the

_____.

testicles

127

953

Orchid/algia means pain in the testicle. Orchid/ectomy means * _____ _____ .

excision of a testicle

954

Around the time of birth the testicles normally descend from the abdominal cavity into the scrotum. Sometimes this fails to happen (crypt/orchid/ism). Surgical repair is indicated. The operation is called an

_____ / ___ / _____ / _____ .

orchid/o/plast/y
orchidoplasty
or' kid o plas ti

955

Build a word meaning:
  fixation of a testicle

_____ / ___ / _____ / _____

  herniation near a testicle

_____ / ___ / _____

  incision into a testicle

_____ / _____

orchid/o/pex/y
orchidopexy
or' kid o peks i
orchidocele
or' ki do sel
orchidotomy
or kid ot' o mi

956

Crypt/orchid/ism means undescended testicle. **Crypt** means hidden. When a testicle is hidden in the abdominal cavity, the condition is known as

_____ / _____ / _____ .

crypt/orchid/ism
cryptorchidism
kript or' kid izm

957

A crypt/ic remark is one with a hidden meaning. A crypt/ic belief is one whose meaning is

_____ .

hidden

958

A crypt/o/gram is writing in code. Crypt/o/toxic means having toxins (poisons) whose action is

_____ .

unknown or
hidden

959

A crypt is a hidden gland or follicle. Build a word meaning:
  inflammation of a crypt

_____ / _____

  excision of a crypt

_____ / _____

cryptitis
krip ti' tis

cryptectomy
krip tek' to mi

128

960

When an organ contains pus that is concealed (hidden), it is said to be

cryptopyic

_____ / _____ / _____ / ic .

961

Excessive secretion (flow) of an endocrine (hidden) gland is called

crypt/orrhea
cryptorrhea
krip to re' a

_____ / _____ .

Work Review Sheets 22 and 23.

962

Colp/o is used in words about the vagina. Colpitis means

inflammation of the vagina

* _____ .

963

Colp/o/dynia means ** _____

vaginal pain
colp/o/path/y
colpopathy
kol pop' a thi

_____ . Any disease of the vagina is called

_____ / _____ / _____ .

964

A colp/o/spasm is a ** _____

vaginal spasm
colp/ectomy
colpectomy
kol pek' to mi

_____ . Excision of a part of the vagina is a

_____ / _____ .

965

Build a word meaning:
   prolapse of the vagina

colpoptosis

_____ / _____ / _____

   fixation of the vagina

colpopexy

_____ / _____ / _____

   surgical repair of the vagina

colpoplasty
(You pronounce)

_____ / _____ / _____

966

Build a word meaning:
   suture of the vagina

colporrhaphy

_____ / _____

   instrument for examining the vagina

colposcope

_____ / _____ / _____

   incision into the vagina

colpotomy
(You pronounce)

_____ / _____

129

The following chart is for use in building words through Frame 992.

COMBINING FORM OF LOCATION	MEANING
ect/o	outer–outside
end/o	inner–inside
mes/o	middle
retr/o	backward–behind
par/a	around–near

967

The blast/o/derm is an embryonic disc of cells that gives rise to the three main layers of tissue in man. The outer germ layer is called the ect/o/derm. The inner germ layer is called the

end/o/derm
endoderm
en' do derm

_____ / _____ / _____.

968

Between the ectoderm and endoderm is a middle germ layer called the

mes/o/derm
mesoderm
mes' o derm

_____ / _____ / _____.

969

The ectoderm forms the skin. The nervous system arises from the same layer as the skin. This layer is the _____.

ectoderm
ek' to derm

970

Sense organs and some glands are also formed from the _____.

ectoderm

971

The end/o/derm forms organs inside the body. The stomach and small intestine arise from the

endoderm

_____ / _____ / _____.

972

The lungs are also formed by the

endoderm

_____.

130

973

The mesoderm forms the organs that arise between the ectoderm and endoderm. Muscles are formed by the _____ .

mesoderm

974

Bones and cartilages also arise from the

_____ .

mesoderm

975

The blastoderm gives rise to the three germ layers. They are:

outer   outer _____ .

mesoderm middle _____ .

endoderm inner _____ .

976

The ectoderm, mesoderm, and endoderm form everything that is in the body.

outer   Ect/o means _____ .

inner   End/o means _____ .

middle Mes/o means _____ .

977

Something produced within an organism is said to be end/o/genous. Something produced outside an organism is

ect/o/genous
ectogenous
ek toj' in us

          /   /

_____ .

978

Ect/o/cyt/ic is an adjective meaning outside a cell. An adjective meaning inside a bladder is

end/o/cyst/ic
endocystic
en' do sis tic

     /   /   /

_____ .

979

Prot/o/plasm is the substance of life. The protoplasm that forms the outer limit of the cell is called

ectoplasm

     /   /

_____ . The protoplasm

endoplasm
(You pronounce)

within the cell is called

     /   /

_____ .

980

End/o/crani/al is an adjective meaning within the cranium. An adjective meaning within cartilage is

end/o/chondr/al
end o kon' dral

     /   /   /

_____ .

981

End/o/enter/itis means inflammation of the lining of the small intestine. Build a word meaning:

pertaining to the lining of the heart (adjective)

_____ / _____ / _____

inflammation of the lining of the colon

_____ / _____ / _____

endocardial or
endocardiac

endocolitis
(You pronounce)

Note the involved development of the word ectopic. (out of place)

ect/o —outside

top/os—place (Greek word)

ic—adjectival suffix

982

An ectopic pregnancy occurs outside of the uterus. A heart on the right side of the body is an

_____ heart.

ectopic
ek top' ik

983

If endometrium occurs in the fallopian tubes, a fertilized egg can lodge in it, thus causing pregnancy. This is an _____ pregnancy.

ectopic

984

An embryo's development in the abdominal cavity is also an _____ pregnancy.

ectopic

985

Think of the meaning while you analyze:

mesoneuritis _____

mesocolic _____

mesocephalic _____

mesocardia _____

mes/o/neur/itis
mes/o/col/ic
mes/o/cephal/ic
mes/o/cardi/a

986

Build an adjective meaning:

behind the colon

_____ / _____ / _____

behind the mammary (gland)

_____ / _____ / mammary

behind the stern/um

_____ / _____ / al

retr/o/col/ic
re tro kol' ik

retr/o/mammary
re tro mam' ma ri

retr/o/stern/al
re tro ster' nal

132

987

Ante/version means turning forward. The word for turning backward is

retroversion
(You pronounce)

_____ / ____ / _____ .

988

The retr/o/periton/eum is the space _____ the peritoneum. An inflammation of this space is called

behind

retr/o/periton/itis
re tro per i to ni' tis

_____ / ____ / _____ / _____ .

989

Ant/e/flexion means forward bending. Retr/o/flexion means ** _____

backward bending

_____ .

990

Par/a/centr/al means

near the center or
around the center

** _____ .

Par/a-/appendic/itis means ** _____

inflammation around
the appendix

_____ .

991

Build a word meaning:
    inflammation around the bladder

paracystitis
par a sis ti' tis

_____ / ____ / _____ / _____

    inflammation of tissues around the vagina

paracolpitis
par a kol pi' tis

_____ / ____ / _____ / _____

992

Build a word meaning inflammation of tissues:

parahepatitis
paranephritis
parapleuritis
(You pronounce)

    around the liver   _____
    around the kidney   _____
    around the pleur/a _____

993

outer
inner
middle
around (near)
behind

Ect/o   means _____ .
End/o   means _____ .
Mes/o   means _____ .
Par/a   means _____ .
Retr/o   means _____ .

994

Aut/o is a word root–combining form that means self. You already recognize **auto** in such ordinary English words as aut/o/mobile (a self-propelled vehicle) and aut/o/bi/o/graph/y. Aut/o means

self

_____ .

133

995

Aut/o/di/a/gnos/is means diagnosing one's own diseases. Aut/o/derm/ic pertains to dermoplasty with

one's own skin

** _____ .

996

Aut/o/nom/ic means self-controlling. Aut/o/lys/is means

self-destruction or
self-destroying

** _____ .

997

aut/o/phob/ia
autophobia
aw to fo' bi a

Aut/o/phag/ia means biting one's self. A word that means abnormal fear of being alone is

_____ / _____ / _____ .

998

aut/o/hem/o/therap/y
aut/o/psych/osis
aut/o/plast/y
(You pronounce)

In the blanks provided, analyze the following:

autohemotherapy _____

autopsychosis _____

autoplasty _____

999

aut/o/phob/ia
aut/o/phag/ia
aut/o/nephr/ectomy
(You pronounce)

When you analyze a word, think of its meaning. If you have forgotten a part of the word, look it up. Analyze:

autophobia _____

autophagia _____

autonephrectomy _____

1000

Mon/o means one or single. You know it in the ordinary English words monotony, monopoly, and monogamy. Whenever you see mon/o, you think of

one

_____ .

1001

one

A mon/o/graph deals with a single subject. A mon/o/nucle/ar cell has _____ nucleus.

1002

mon/o/cyt/e
mon/oma
(You pronounce)

Mon/o/man/ia is insanity on one subject only. Build a word meaning:

one cell _____ / _____ / _____

one tumor _____ / _____

1003

Analyze the following words:

monomyoplegia _____

mononeural _____

mononucleosis _____

mon/o/my/o/pleg/ia
mon/o/neur/al
mon/o/nucle/osis
(You pronounce)

1004

Mult/i means the opposite of mon/o. Mult/i means

** _____ .

many or more than one

1005

In ordinary English, you are acquainted with multi in the words multiply and multitude. Something composed of multiple parts has _____ parts.

many

1006

Something that is mult/i/capsular has

* _____ .

many capsules

1007

Mult/i/glandular means

* _____ .

Mult/i/cellular means

* _____ .

Mult/i/nuclear means

* _____ .

many glands

many cells

many nuclei

1008

A mult/i/par/a is a woman who has born more than one child. Par/o is the word root–combining form for bear. Mult/i/par/ous is the adjectival form of _____ / _____ / _____ / _____ .

mult/i/par/a
multipara
mul tip' a ra

1009

Mult/i/par/a **always** refers to the mother. Mult/i/par/ous may refer to the mother or may mean multiple birth (twins or triplets). When desiring to indicate that a woman has born more than one child, use the noun

_____ / _____ / _____ / _____ .

multipara

1010

multipara

multiparous

mul tip' ar ous

Multiparous is the adjectival form of _____.
To indicate that twins are born, say

_____ / ___ / _____ / _____ birth.

1011

To indicate that triplets are born, say

multiparous

_____ birth. If
ten children were born, you would still use the
adjective

multiparous

_____.

1012

Null/i means none. To nullify something is to bring
it to nothing. There are not many medical words
using null/i; but when you do see it, it means

_____.

1013

a woman who has never
born a child

A null/i/par/a is

**

_____.

1014

Analyze the following:

null/i/par/a

   nullipara _____

                            (noun)

null/i/par/ous

   nulliparous _____

null/i/par/ity

(You pronounce)

                      (adjective)

   nulliparity _____

                           (noun)

1015

Give the word root–combining form for:

null/i

   none _____ / ___

mon/o

   one (single) _____ / ___

mult/i

   many _____ / ___

par/o

   bear _____ / ___

Work Review Sheets 24 and 25.

PREFIXES OF PLACE

These prefixes often cause difficulty in word building because of their similarity. The explanations should be helpful. These forms will probably require extra work. This is your first introduction to prefixes of place. Use this information **carefully** while working through frame 1040.

PREFIX	MEANING	SENSE OF MEANING
ab	from	away from
de	from	down from or from—resulting in less than
ex	from	out from

1016
You have already learned **ab** as the opposite of **ad**.
from   **ad** means toward. **ab** means _____.

1017
Ab/duct/ion means moving away from the mid-line. Ab/norm/al means going
away from   * _____ the normal.

1018
Ab/or/al means away from the mouth. Ab/errant
away from   means wandering * _____
the normal course.

1019
An ab/irritant is something that takes pain
away from   * _____ the patient. Ab/
lact/ation means taking the baby
away from   * _____ the breast.

1020
Ab/ort means taking the fetus
away from   * _____ the mother. To ab/
rade the skin is to scrape skin
away from   * _____ the patient.

137

1021

Analyze the words:

abduct _____

abneural _____

abmortal _____

ab/duct
ab/neur/al
ab/mort/al
(You pronounce)

1022

de is another prefix that means _____.

from

1023

When one de/scends the stairs, he comes down from a higher level. A de/scending nerve track comes *_____ the brain.

down from

1024

A de/scending nerve track carries descending impulses *_____ the brain.

down from

1025

Deciduous leaves fall from a tree. "Baby teeth" that fall from a child's mouth are called

_____ teeth.

deciduous
de sid' u us

1026

A de/coction is made by boiling down a fluid. While a de/coction is boiling down to a thicker substance, water is being taken _____ it.

from

1027

When water is taken from a substance, the substance is less than it was. De/hydr/ation takes water _____ something.

from

1028

When water is taken from prunes, de/hydr/ation occurs. When water is taken from a cell,

_____ / _____ / _____ also

occurs.

de/hydr/ation
dehydration
de hi dra' shun

1029

When something is de/hydr/ated, it is less than it was. When water is lost from the body due to excessive vomiting, the patient is

_____ / _____ / _____.

de/hydr/ated
de hi' dra ted

1030

Vomiting can cause dehydration. A high fever can also cause _____.

dehydration

138

1031

When calcium is removed from the bones, there is less calcium than formerly. This process is called

_____ / calcification _____ .

decalcification
de kal si fi ka' shun

1032

Decalcification can occur from many causes. When a pregnant woman does not eat enough calcium for the growing baby, her own bones will be robbed of calcium; and

_____

will occur.

decalcification

1033

Since vitamin D helps control calcium metabolism, inadequate vitamin D in the diet can account for some _____ .

Parathyroid imbalance can also cause

_____ .

decalcification

decalcification

1034

ex also means from, but in the sense of

＊_____ .

(Refer to page 137.)

out from

1035

Ex/eresis means the taking out (from) any part of the body. To excise is to cut _____ and remove a part.

out

1036

To exhale is to breathe out waste matter

_____ the body.

from

1037

Ex/cretion is the process of **ex**pelling (or getting out from the body) a substance. Expelling urine is urinary _____ .

excretion
(You pronounce)

1038

Expelling carbon dioxide is called respiratory _____ . Expelling sweat is dermal

_____ .

excretion
excretion

1039

Expelling menses is menstrual _____ .

Expelling fecal matter is gastrointestinal

_____ .

excretion

excretion

139

1040

Try to work this summary frame without referring to page 137. Give the prefix meaning **from** in the following sense:

ab

ex

de

away from _____

out from _____

down from or from, resulting in less than

_____

1041

Narc/o is the word root–combining form for sleep. A narc/o/tic is a drug that produces sleep. Opium produces sleep. Opium is a

narc/o/tic
narcotic
nar kot' ic

_____ / _____ / _____ .

1042

A narcotic should be used only when advised by a physician. Codeine produces sleep. Codeine is a

narcotic

_____ .

1043

narcotic

Laudanum is also a _____ .

1044

Since narcotics can also cause addiction, a physician must have a narcotic license in order to dispense or write for _____
(plural).

narcotics

1045

narc/osis
narcosis
nar ko' sis

The **condition** induced by narcotics is called

_____ / _____ .

1046

Narc/o/leps/y means seizure or attacks of sleep. When a person is absolutely unable to stay awake, he suffers from

narc/o/leps/y
narcolepsy
nar' ko lep si

_____ / _____ / _____ / _____ .

1047

Narcolepsy is uncontrollable. A person may fall sound asleep standing at a bus stop. This is

narcolepsy

_____ .

1048

A cerebroma, cerebral arteriosclerosis, and paresis are some causes of sleep seizures which are called

narcolepsy

_____ .

1049

Narc/o any place in a word makes you think of

sleep

_____.

1050

Is/o is used in words to mean equal. Something

equal

that is is/o/metr/ic is of _____ di-

mensions.

1051

Something that is is/o/cell/ular is composed of

equal

_____ cells.

1052

An is/o/ton/ic solution has the same osmotic

is/o/ton/ic
isotonic
i so ton' ic

pressure as red blood cells. Blood serum is an

___/___/_____/_____ solution.

1053

Intr/a/ven/ous glucose is another

isotonic

___/___/_____/_____ solution.

1054

Any solution that will not destroy red blood cells

because of pressure difference is an

isotonic

_____ solution.

1055

Build a word meaning:

fingers or toes of equal length

isodactylism

___/___/_____/ ism

pertaining to equal temperature

isothermal (or ic)
(You pronounce)

___/___/_____/

1056

an is a prefix meaning without. Something that is

without equality is unequal. The combining form

an/is/o or
anis/o

for unequal is ___/___.

1057

Anis/o/cor/ia means that the pupils of the eyes are

unequal

of _____ size.

1058

Anis/o/mast/ia means that a woman's breasts are

unequal

of _____ size.

1059

Anis/o/cyt/osis means that cells are of unequal sizes. This word is commonly limited to red blood cells in medical usage. A word indicating a condition of inequality in cell size is

_____ / _____ / _____ / _____ .

anis/o/cyt/osis
anisocytosis
an i so si to' sis

1060

Normal red blood cells are the same size (7.2 microns). An abnormal condition resulting in unequal size of red blood cells is

_____ .

anisocytosis

1061

Red blood cells are formed in the bone marrow. An unhealthy bone marrow can result in unequal red blood cells or

_____ .

anisocytosis

1062

Lack of hemoglobin can also cause

_____ .

anisocytosis

Use the following information to work Frames 1063 through 1082. This is another group of prefixes of place.

PREFIX	MEANING	DIFFERENTIATION
di/a	through	Used with the word root–combining forms you know. More medical
per	through	Prefix from Latin. Used in ordinary English
peri	around	Prefix from Greek used with the word root–combining forms you know. More medical
circum	around	Latin prefix used in ordinary English

1063

Peri/articular means around articulations or joints. Peri/tonsill/ar means

*_____ .

around the tonsil

1064

Peri/col/ic means

*_____ .

around the colon or
pertaining to around
the colon

1065

Peri/dent/al means around a tooth. A word that means around a cartilage is

peri/chondr/al
perichondral
per i kon' dral

_____ / _____ / _____ .

1066

Build a word meaning:

    inflammation around a gland

periadenitis

_____ / _____ / _____

    inflammation around the vagina

pericolpitis

_____ / _____ / _____

    inflammation around the liver

perihepatitis

_____ / _____ / _____

    excision of tissue around the heart

pericardiectomy
(You pronounce)

_____ / _____ / _____

1067

Another prefix that means around is

circum

_____ .

1068

Circum/ocular means _____ the eyes.

around

1069

Circum/or/al means _____ the mouth.

around

1070

Circum/scribed means limited in space (as though a line were drawn around it). A hive is limited in space—does not spread. A hive may be called a

circumscribed
sir' kum scrib d

_____ wheal.

1071

A boil is also limited in the space it covers. A boil is a _____ lesion.

circumscribed

1072

Pimples and pustules are also

circumscribed

_____ lesions.

1073

Moving toward is ad/duct/ion.
Moving away is ab/duct/ion.
Moving around (circular motion) is

circum/duct/ion
circumduction
sir kum duk' shun

_____ / _____ / _____ .

143

1074

There are two prefixes that mean through. The one that you would expect to use more often in medical

di/a

terminology is ___/___.

1075

You have already learned di/a/gnos/is which means

through

knowing _____, and di/a/ therm/y which means heating

through

_____.

1076

Build a word meaning:
  flowing through (drop the o)

di/a/rrhea

___/___/_____.

di/a/therm/al
/ic

pertaining to heating through
___/___/___.

1077

Per/for/ation (noun) means puncturing

through

_____.

1078

To per/for/ate means to puncture or make a hole

through

_____.

1079

The past tense of per/for/ate is per/for/ated. An ulcer that has eaten through the stomach wall has

perforated

_____ (past tense) it.

1080

perforate

Ulcers can also _____ (present tense) the duodenum.

1081

When ulcers perforate an organ, a

perforation

___/___/ation ___ (noun) is formed.

1082

Percussion (noun) means a striking through. Read the section on percussion in your dictionary. Analyze the word here.

per/cuss/ion
percussion

___/___/_____.

144

1083

Summarize:

Two prefixes meaning through are _____ and

_____ / ___ .

Two prefixes meaning around are

_____ and _____ .

per and di/a

circum and peri

1084

Necr/o is used in words pertaining to death. Necr/o/cyt/osis is cellular _____ .

death

1085

A necr/o/meter measures _____ organs.

dead

1086

A necr/o/parasite is one that lives on

_____ organic matter.

dead

1087

Necr/osis refers to a condition in which dead tissue is surrounded with healthy tissue. Certain diseases can cause _____ / _____ of the bones.

necr/osis
necrosis
nek ro' sis

1088

When blood supply is cut off from an arm, gangrene sets in. This results in

_____ (death) of the arm tissue.

necrosis

1089

When gangrene occurs anywhere in the body,

_____ is seen.

necrosis

1090

Build a word meaning:

excision of dead tissue

_____ / _____ .

necr/ectomy

incision into (dissection of) a dead body

_____ / _____ .

necr/otomy

abnormal fear of death

_____ / ___ / _____ .

necr/o/phob/ia
(You pronounce)

1091

There are two ways of saying post-mortem (after death) examination. One is aut/o/psy. The other is

_____ / ___ / psy ___ .

necr/o/psy
necropsy
nek' rop si

145

1092

abnormal or
unusual

Phil/ia is the opposite of phob/ia. Phobia is abnormal fear of. Philia is ** _____
attraction to.

1093

abnormal attraction
to dead bodies

Necr/o/phob/ia is an abnormal fear of dead bodies.
Necr/o/phil/ia is
* _____ .

1094

Words that can end in phob/ia, can end in phil/ia.
Abnormal fear of water is

hydrophobia

_____ / __ / _____ / _____ .

hydr/o/phil/ia
hi dro fil' i a

Abnormal attraction to water is

_____ / __ / _____ / _____ .

1095

Think of the meaning while building words opposite
to

    hemat/o/phob/ia

hematophilia

_____ / __ / _____ / _____

    pyr/o/phob/ia

pyrophilia

_____ / __ / _____ / _____

    aer/o/phob/ia

aerophilia

_____ / __ / _____ / _____

autophilia
(You pronounce)

    aut/o/phob/ia

_____ / __ / _____ / _____

1096

attraction to
liking
loving

Phil/o is the word root–combining form which
means ** _____
_____ .

1097

philosopher
philosophy
philology
etc.

Can you think of a nonmedical word that involves
phil/o? If so, write it here.

_____

Work Review Sheets 26 and 27.

1098

Hom/o in words means same. Hom/o/genized
milk has the same amount of cream throughout.
Hom/o/gland/ular means pertaining to the

same gland

* _____ .

146

1099

Hom/o/therm/al means having the _____ body temperature.

same

1100

Hom/o/later/al means pertaining to the
_____ side.

same

1101

Hom/o/sex/ual means abnormal attraction to the same sex. When men are attracted to men much more than to women, they are said to be
_____ / _____ / _____ / _____.

hom/o/sex/ual
homosexual
ho mo sex' u al

1102

When women are attracted to women rather than to men, they too are called
_____.

homosexual

1103

Heter/o is the opposite of hom/o. Heter/o means
** _____.

different

1104

Heter/opia means_____ vision in each eye.

different

1105

Heter/o/trich/osis means having hair of many _____ colors.

different

1106

Look up the meaning of homogeneous and hetero-geneous in your dictionary. Understand and know these words.

Analyze them here.
_____ / _____ / _____ / _____
_____ / _____ / _____ / _____

hom/o/gene/ous
ho mo je' ne us
heter/o/gene/ous
het er o je' ne us

1107

Think of the meaning while you form **opposites** of the following:

hom/o/lys/is
_____ / _____ / _____ / _____

heter/o/lys/is

hom/o/genesis
_____ / _____ / _____

heter/o/genesis

hom/o/sex/ual
_____ / _____ / _____ / _____

heter/o/sex/ual

147

1108

Splen/o is used in words about the spleen. Build a word meaning:

excision of the spleen

splen/ectomy
sple nek' to mi

_____/_____

enlargement of the spleen

splen/o/megal/y

_____/___/_____/___

prolapse of the spleen

splen/o/ptosis
(You pronounce)

_____/___/_____

1109

Build a word meaning:

surgical fixation of the spleen

splenopexy

_____/___/_____/___

any disease of the spleen

splenopathy

_____/___/_____/___

suture of the spleen

splenorrhaphy

_____/_____

hemorrhage from the spleen

splenorrhagia

_____/_____

1110

The spleen is one of the blood-forming organs. **Splen/algia** means

pain in the spleen

_____******_____.

1111

Splen/ic means

pertaining to the spleen

_____******_____.

1112

syn and **sym** are different forms of the same pre-

together or joined

fix. syn and sym mean _____
(Frame 816 if you have forgotten).

1113

You have already learned **syn** in the words syn-dactylism, synergetic, synarthrosis, and syndrome. (Review Frames 816 through 823.)

1114

syn is the form of the prefix that is used to mean fixed or joined, except when it is followed by **b, m,**

sym

or **p.** Then _____ is used.

148

1115

Sympathy is an ordinary word that has a special medical meaning. Read this meaning in your medical dictionary. From either a medical or Webster's dictionary, find what it takes to fill this blank: sym + path/os, the Greek word for

suffering (Taber's)
feeling (Webster's)

_____ .

1116

eyelids have grown together or adhesions of the eyelids

A sym/physis has grown together. Sym/blephar/on means ** _____

_____ .

1117

Build a word meaning:

sympodia

lower extremities are grown together (united)
_____ / pod / ia

sympathectomy

excision of a sympathetic nerve
/ path /
_____

sympathoma
(You pronounce)

tumor of a sympathetic nerve
/ /
_____

1118

symmetry
symmetric
symmetrical

Find a fairly **common** word in your medical dictionary in which **sym** is followed by **m**. (There are only two or three to choose from.) One is
** _____ .

1119

symbol or
symbolism

Find a **common** word in your medical dictionary that is used in ordinary English in which **sym** is followed by **b**. It is ** _____ .

1120

b m p

syn and sym both mean together. **sym** is used when followed by the letters, _____ , _____ , and _____ . syn is used in other medical words.

1121

super and **supra** are both prefixes which mean, respectively, above or beyond. Analyze the following words in which super and supra are used. Think of the meaning of the word as you analyze it. If necessary, consult a dictionary.

149

1122
Super

super/fici/al	superficial	*confined to the surface*
super/cili/ary	superciliary	*pertaining to the region of the brow*
super/infect/ion	superinfection	*new infection by same organism*
super/ior/ity	superiority	*exaggeration of one's ability*
super/leth/al	superlethal	*beyond a fatal limit*
super/numer/ary	supernumerary	*exceeding the regular number*

1123
Supra

supra/lumb/ar	supralumbar	*above lumbar region*
supra/pub/ic	suprapubic	*" pubic arch*
supra/crani/al	supracranial	*upper surface of skull*
supra/ren/al	suprarenal	*above the kidney*
supra/ren/oma	suprarenoma	*tissue tumor above kid*
supra/ren/o/path/y	suprarenopathy	*disease of glands above the kidneys*

If you made a mistake in the division of the word parts following "super," ignore it. If you made a mistake in dividing "supra" words, it is wrong.

1124
In Webster's Collegiate Dictionary (or in any good dictionary) look up words beginning with super. Write the number of columns of words beginning with super in the blank indicated below. Do the same with supra. Now do the same thing with both prefixes using your medical dictionary.

approximately:
5—$\frac{1}{4}$, $\frac{1}{3}$
1$\frac{1}{2}$—3

	super	supra
Webster	⎯⎯	⎯⎯
medical dictionary	⎯⎯	⎯⎯

1125

super is used more frequently in modern English
supra is used more frequently in straight medical words

Draw a conclusion about **super** and **supra** from your answer in the last frame.
super is ** *more frequently in English*.
supra is ** *" " used in medical*.

150

a and **an** are prefixes that mean without.
Examine the following list of words.

an/al/ges/ia *without feeling*   a/bi/o/tic *without life*
an/aph/ia *sensitivity to touch*   a/blast/em/ic' *not germinal*
an/em/ia *without blood*   a/clamp/sia *without spasm*
an/encephal/us " *brain*   a/derm/ia " *skin*
an/esthes/ia " *sensation*   a/febrile " *fever*
an/iso/cyt/osis " *equal cells*   a/galact/ia " *milk*
an/idr/osis *absent from sweat*   a/kinesi/a " *movement*
an/irid/ia *without an iris*   a/lali/a " *speech*
an/onych/ia " *nail*   a/men/a " *menses*
an/op/ia " *vision*   a/pne/a " *breath*
an/ur/ia " *urine completely*   a/reflex/ia " *reflex*
an/ur/esis " *urine partically*   a/seps/is " *infection*

Draw a conclusion.
Use **a** if it is followed by a

_____.

Use **an** if it is followed by a

_____.

(Answers at bottom of page.)

1126
Hyster/o is used in words about the uterus. Metr/o
is another word root–combining form that refers
to the _____.

uterus

1127
Hyster/o **usually** refers to the uterus as an organ.
Metr/o **usually** refers to the tissues of the

_____.

uterus

1128
There are exceptions to the rule, but in general
hyster/o means the uterus as an _____.
Metr/o refers to the uterus in the sense of its _

_____.

organ

tissues

1129
Metr/itis means an inflammation of the uterine
musculature. Metr/o/paralysis means paralysis of
the ** _____.

uterus or
uterine musculature

consonant
vowel

151

1130

Using metr/orrhagia as an example, build a word meaning:

metr/orrhea
met ror re' a

flow or discharge from the uterus

_____/_____

metr/orrhexis
met ro reks' is

rupture of the uterus

_____/_____

1131

Build a word meaning:

metr/o/path/y or
hysteropathy

any uterine disease

_____/___/_____/_____

metr/o/cele or
hysterocele
(You pronounce)

herniation of the uterus

_____/___/_____

1132

The end/o/metr/ium is the lining of the uterus.
Build a word meaning:

end/o/metr/itis
en do me tri' tis

inflammation of the uterine lining

_____/___/_____/_____

end/o/metr/ectomy
en do me trek' to me

excision of the uterine lining

_____/___/_____/_____

More prefixes! Use this chart to work Frames 1133 through 1152.

PREFIX	MEANING	SPECIAL COMMENT
epi	over–upon	
extra	outside of beyond in addition to	
infra	below–under	almost always below a part of the body almost always adjectival in form There are fewer words beginning with **infra** than with **sub**
sub	under–below	Many words of all kinds begin with sub

152

1133

The epi/gastr/ic region is the region

over the stomach
  ＊_____ .

1134

Epi/splen/itis means inflammation of the tissue

over the spleen
  ＊_____ .

1135

Build a word meaning:

inflammation of the area over the bladder

epi/cyst/itis
ep i sis ti' tis
  _____ / _____ / _____

epi/nephr/itis
ep i nef ri' tis

inflammation (of the tissue) upon the kidney
  _____ / _____ / _____

1136

Build a word meaning:

excision of the tissue upon the kidney

epi/nephr/ectomy
ep i ne frek' to mi
  _____ / _____ / _____

epi gastr/orrhaphy
ep i gas tror' a fi

suture of the region over the stomach
  _____ / _____ / _____

1137

Build a word meaning pertaining to

(the tissue) upon the skin

epi/derm/al
　　　　/ic
  _____ / _____ / _____

(the tissue) covering the cranium

epicranial
  _____ / _____ / _____

episternal
(You pronounce)

the area above the stern/um
  _____ / _____ / _____

1138

outside of
or beyond

Extra/nuclear means ＊＊_____
a nucleus.

1139

outside of
or beyond

Extra/uterine means ＊＊_____ the
uterus.

153

1140

Think of the meaning as you analyze:

extra-articular *outside a joint*

extra-/articul/ar
eks tra' ar tic' u lar

_____/_____/_____

extracystic *outside or unrelated the bladder*

extra/cyst/ic
eks tra sis' tic

_____/_____

extradural *outside ,*

extra/dur/al
eks tra dur' ral

_____/_____/_____

1141

Think of the meaning as you analyze:

extragenital *outside gential organs*

extra/genit/al

_____/_____/_____

extrahepatic *outside liver area*

extra/hepat/ic

_____/_____/_____

extramarginal – *Sub-liminal condension (unconscious)*

extra/margin/al
(You pronounce)

_____/_____/_____

1142

adjectives

Look at the words in the last two frames. Draw a conclusion. **extra** is used as a prefix in words that are usually _____ (nouns/adjectives).

1143

below–under

infra is a prefix that means _____.

1144

below or under

Infra/mammary means _____ the mammary gland.

1145

below or under

Infra/patell/ar means _____ the patella (knee-cap).

1146

under or below

sub is a prefix that means _____.

1147

under

Sub/abdominal means _____ the abdomen.

below

Sub/aur/al means _____ the ear.

1148

The prefixes infra and sub are sometimes confusing in word building. For that reason, you will build words that can take either prefix. When you see sub or infra, you will think of _____ or _____ .

under or below

1149

Using stern/o, build two words meaning below the sternum.

_____ / _____ / al

_____ / _____ / _____

A word meaning above the sternum is

supra / _____ / _____ .

infra/stern/al

sub/stern/al

supra/stern/al

1150

Using cost/o, build two words meaning under the ribs.

_____ / _____ / _____

_____ / _____ / _____

A word meaning above the ribs is

_____ / _____ / _____ .

infra/cost/al

sub/cost/al

supra/cost/al

1151

Using pub/o, build two words meaning under the pubis.

_____ / _____ / _____

_____ / _____ / _____

A word meaning above the pubis is

_____ / _____ / _____ .

infra/pub/ic

sub/pub/ic

supra/pub/ic

1152

You have now learned your prefixes of location. You should review them by making a list of them, with their meaning plus anything special about them.

Do it.

1153

Sepsis is a noun meaning reaction against bacteria and their poisons. There must be infection for seps/is to occur. A noun meaning without or free from sepsis is _____ / _____ .

a/seps/is
asepsis
a sep' sis

155

1154

Sept/ic is the adjectival form of sepsis. The adjectival form for the word meaning free from infection is ____/____ .

a/sept/ic
aseptic
a sep' tic

1155

Sept/emia is an infection in the bloodstream. Sept/o/py/emia means ** _____ _____ .

infection with
pus in the
bloodstream

1156

Study the last two frames. A word root–combining form for infection is _____/_____ .

sept/o (used most)
or seps/o

1157

Tabulate the material from Frames 1153 to 1156.

noun for infected _____/_____

seps/is

adjective for infected _____/_____

sept/ic

noun for free from infection
_____/_____ _____/_____

a/seps/is

adjective for free from infection
_____/_____ _____/_____

a/sept/ic

1158

anti is a prefix that means against. An anti/pyretic is an agent that works _____ a fever.

against

1159

An anti/narcotic is an agent that works _____ narcotics.

against

1160

An anti/mycotic is an agent that works _____ fungus infections.

against

1161

Build an adjective describing the agent that works against:

rheumatic disease
_____/_____

anti/rheumatic

spastic disease
_____/_____

anti/spastic

syphilitic infections
_____/_____

anti/syphilitic
(You pronounce)

1162

Build an adjective describing the agent that works against:

    convulsive states

anticonvulsive

_____ / _____

    arthritic diseases

antiarthritic

_____ / _____

    toxic states

antitoxic
(You pronounce)

_____ / _____

1163

The adjective denoting a drug that works against infection is

antiseptic
an ti sep' tik

_____ / _____ / _____ .

1164

contra is a prefix that also means against. contra is used with modern English words. To contra/dict someone is to speak _____

against

what he is saying.

1165

Contra/ry things are _____ each

against

other. A contra/ry person is usually one who is

against

_____ your wishes.

1166

In medical terminology, contra is mainly confined in use to four words. However, in these four words

against

contra still means _____ .

1167

Analyze these four words:

    contraindication

contra/indicat/ion

_____ / _____ / _____

    contraceptive

contra/cept/ive

_____ / _____ / _____

    contravolitional

contra/volition/al

_____ / _____ / _____

    contralateral

contra/later/al
(You pronounce)

_____ / _____ / _____

Don't count it wrong if you miss the second diagonal. (If you get it right, you should feel good.)

1168

Using the words in Frame 1167 fill the following blanks with a word whose literal meaning is:

against volition _____

against indication _____

against conception _____

against the side _____

contravolitional
contraindication
contraceptive
contralateral
(You pronounce)

1169

Using these same words and a medical dictionary, if necessary, fill the blanks with the word that covers the more extended meaning:

device to prevent conception _____

pertaining to the opposite side _____

against the will _____

symptom makes inadvisable _____

contraceptive
contralateral
contravolitional
contraindication
(You pronounce)

1170

Using the noun given, build the other parts of the same word:

contra/ / indicat/ / ion (noun)

_____ (verb)

_____ / _____ / _____ (past tense)

contra/indicat/e
contra/indicat/ed
(You pronounce)

1171

trans is a prefix meaning across or over. To trans/ port a cargo is to carry it _____ the ocean or land.

across or over

1172

Trans/position means literally position

_____.

across or over

1173

Transposition means literally placed across. When an organ is placed across to the other side of the body (from where it normally is found)

_____ / _____.

occurs.

trans/position
transposition
trans po zi' shun

1174

Cardi/ac transposition means that the heart is on the right side of the body. If the stomach is on the right side of the body, the condition is gastr/ic

_____.

transposition

158

1175

The liver belongs on the right side of the body. If a patient's liver is on the left side of the body, the condition is hepat/ic _____.

transposition

1176

If the spleen is on the opposite side of the body, the condition is splen/ic _____. If the pancreas is on the opposite side of the body, use the word pancreat/ic _____.

transposition

transposition

1177

When a trans/fusion is given, blood is passed _____ from one person to another.

across or over

1178

Analyze:

transillumination _____

transvaginal _____

transthoracic _____

transurethral _____

trans/illumin/ation
trans/vagin/al
trans/thorac/ic
trans/urethr/al
(You pronounce)

1179

Transpiration is the act of carrying water vapors across lung or skin tissue to eliminate them from the body. Breathing is respiration. Breathing consists of the following two processes: expiration and inspiration. Think of the meaning as you analyze:

expiration

_____ / _____ / _____

inspiration

_____ / _____ / _____

ex/pir/ation

in/spir/ation

1180

Look at the words in Frame 1179. The word that means to breathe **in** is _____.

inspiration

1181

in is a prefix that means in or not. In/compatible drugs are drugs that do _____ mix with each other.

not

1182

In/compet/ency occurs in an organ when it is _____ able to perform its function.

not

159

1183

In/compet/ency is a noun. When the ile/o/cec/al valve cannot perform its function, the result is ileocecal

_____ / _____ / _____ .

in/compet/ency
incompetency
in com' pe ten si

1184

When blood seeps back through the aortic valves, call it aortic

_____ .

incompetency

1185

When a person is not able to take care of himself, you may call it ment/al

_____ . You may

even say the person is mentally

_____ (adjective).

incompetency

incompetent

1186

in is a prefix that means _____ or _____ .

in or not

1187

To in/cis/e is to cut into. This is a verb. The noun from in/cis/e is _____ / _____ / _____ .

in/cis/ion
incision
in sizh' un

1188

itis is the suffix for

_____ / _____ .

in/flammation
inflammation
in fle ma' shun

1189

Analyze:

inject _____

injected _____

injector _____

injection _____

in/ject
in/ject/ed
in/ject/or
in/ject/ion
(Do you know the
meaning?)
(You pronounce)

1190

In Frame 1189 the prefix **in** means _____ .

in

1191

Analyze:

insane _____ / _____

insomnia

_____ / _____

insanitary

_____ / _____

in/sane

in/somnia

in/sanitary
(You pronounce)

160

1192

not

In Frame 1191, the prefix **in** means _____.

Work Review Sheets 28 and 29.

1193

Mal is a French word that means bad. **mal** is also a prefix that means bad or poor. Mal/odor/ous means having a _____ odor.

bad

1194

poorly formed or
poor formation

Mal/aise means a general feeling of illness or poor feeling. Mal/form/ation means **_____

_____.

1195

poor nutrition
bad (abnormal)

position or
placement

Mal/nutrition means
          **_____.

Mal/position means
          **_____.

1196

mal/aria
malaria
ma la' ri a

Before people knew that mosquitoes carry malaria, they thought this disease was caused by bad air. Analyze malaria. _____

1197

mal/ari/al
mal/ari/ous
mal/ari/o/log/y
mal/ari/o/therap/y
(You pronounce)

Analyze these words involving the disease malaria:
    malarial   _____
    malarious   _____
    malariology   _____
    malariotherapy _____

1198

malari/o

Look at the words in the last two frames. Now find the word root–combining form for the disease malaria. _____ / _____

1199

At the top of the next page is a chart that shows some of the prefixes of quantity. Use it while working Frames 1200 through 1216.

161

PREFIX	MEANING	EXPLANATION
uni	one	
bi	two double	
tri	three	
semi	half	Used with modern English words or words closer to modern English
hemi	half	used more with straight medical words

1200

The tri/ceps muscle has _____ heads. — three

A tri/cusp/id valve has _____ cusps. — three

The tri/gemin/al nerve has _____ branches. — three

1201

A bi/cusp/id is a tooth with _____ cusps. — two

Bi/foc/al glasses have _____ foci in one lens. — two

A bi/furc/ation has _____ forks or branches. — two

1202

A uni/corn has _____ horn. — one

Uni/ov/al pertains to twins who develop from _____ ovum. Uni/vers/al means combined into _____ whole. — one / one

1203

Later/al means pertaining to the side. Build a word meaning pertaining to:

one side

_____ / _____ / _____ — uni/later/al

two sides

_____ / _____ / _____ — bi/later/al

three sides

_____ / _____ / _____ — tri/later/al (You pronounce)

1204

A tri/later/al figure looks like this △. You call this a _____ / _____ . — tri/angle

1205

Mult/i/cell/ular means made of many cells. Build a word meaning:

made of two cells

bi/cell/ular

_____ / _____ / _____

uni/cell/ular
(You pronounce)

made of one cell only

_____ / _____ / _____

1206

Some cells are mult/i/nucle/ar in nature. Build a word meaning:

having one nucle/us

uni/nucle/ar

_____ / _____ / _____

bi/nucle/ar
(You pronounce)

having two nucle/i

_____ / _____ / _____

1207

Mult/i/para refers to a woman who has had more than one child. Build a word meaning:

uni/para
u nip' a ra

a woman who has had one child

_____

bi/para
bip' a ra

a woman who has had two children

_____

tri/para
trip' a ra

a woman who has had three children

_____

1208

bi/furc/ates
bifurcates
bi fur' kates

To bi/furc/ate is to divide into two forks. When an artery divides into two, it

_____ / _____ / _____ (s) .

1209

bifurcation
bi fur ka' shun

Bifurcate is a verb. The noun is bifurcation. When a nerve divides into two branches, a

_____ (noun) is

formed.

1210

bifurcations
(You pronounce)

Various ducts in the body also form

_____ (noun–

plural).

1211

one
two
three
many

uni means _____ .

bi means _____ .

tri means _____ .

Mult/i means _____ .

163

1212

semi and hemi

There are two prefixes that mean half. They are
_____ and _____ .

1213

Form a word that means:
half circle

semi/circle

_____/_____

half conscious

semi/conscious

_____/_____

semi/private
(You pronounce)

half private

_____/_____

1214

Build a word meaning:
having only half a heart (noun)

hemi/cardi/a

_____/_____/_____

removal of half the stomach

hemi/gastr/ectomy
hemi/pleg/ia
(hemi/paralysis)
(You pronounce)

_____/_____/_____

paralysis of half the body

_____/_____/ ia

1215

Build a word meaning:
half circular

semi/circular

_____

half normal

semi/normal

_____

semi/comatose
(You pronounce)

half comatose

_____

1216

Build a word with the literal meaning of:
half atrophy

hemi/a/troph/y

_____/_____/_____

half hypertrophy

hemi/hyper/troph/y

_____/_____/_____

hemi/dys/troph/y
(You pronounce)

half dystrophy

_____/_____/_____

1217

with

con is a prefix that means **with.** Con/genit/al
means born _____ .

164

1218

A child with con/genit/al cataracts is

born with

_____ * _____ cataracts.

1219

There are many con/genit/al deformities. A child born with a lateral curvature of the spine has a

con/genit/al
congenital
con jen' i tal

_____ / _____ / _____ scoliosis.

1220

Another way of saying born with deformity is to say congenital anomaly. A child born humpbacked has

congenital

a _____ anomaly.

1221

A child born with hydr/ophthalm/os has

congenital

_____ glaucoma.

1222

A child born with syphilis has

congenital

_____ syphilis.

1223

con —prefix—with
sanguin/o —combining form—blood
ity —noun suffix

Using what you need of the above word parts, build a word meaning literally with blood or in usage blood relationship.

con/sanguin/ity
consanguinity
kon san gwin' it i

_____ / _____ / _____

1224

Con/sanguin/ity is a relationship by descent from a common ancestor. The noun that expresses the relationship of cousins is

consanguinity

_____ .

1225

The relationship of second cousins is that of

consanguinity

_____ .

1226

Sanguin/o means bloody. Build a word meaning pertaining to blood.

sanguin/al
sang' gwin al

_____ / _____

1227

dis is a prefix that means **to free of** or **to undo**. Dis/ease means literally

to free of ease

_____ ** _____ .

165

1228

To dis/sect is to cut a tissue or to undo it (into parts) for purposes of study. Analyze:

dis/sect

dissect

_____

dissection

dis/sect/ion

_____

dis/sect/ed
(You pronounce)

dissected

_____

1229

dis/infect
dis/infect/ant
dis/infect/ion
dis/infect/ed
(You pronounce)

To dis/infect is to free of infection. Analyze:

disinfect _____

disinfectant _____

disinfection _____

disinfected _____

1230

To dis/associate from reality is to be mentally ill. Analyze:

dis/associate
dis/sociate
dis/sociated
dis/sociation

disassociate _____

dissociate _____

dissociated _____

dissociation _____

1231

dis is a prefix that means

to free of—to undo
with

*_____.

con is a prefix that means _____.

Use the following chart to work Frames 1232 through 1240.

PREFIX	MEANING	
post	behind after	
ante	before forward	few usages
pre	before in front of	many usages

166

1232

after

behind

Post/cibal means _____ meals.

Post/esophageal means _____ the esophagus.

1233

before

in front of

Pre/an/esthetic means _____ anesthesia.

Pre/hyoid means *_____ the hyoid bone.

1234

before

forward

Ante/pyretic means _____ the fever.

Ante/flexion means _____ bending.

1235

Nat/al means birth. Think of the meaning while you analyze:

post/nat/al
pre/nat/al
ante/nat/al
(You pronounce)

postnatal _____

prenatal _____

antenatal _____

1236

Febr/ile means fever. Think of the meaning while you analyze:

post/febr/ile
post fe' bril
ante/febr/ile
an te feb' ril

postfebrile _____

antefebrile _____

1237

Mortem means death. What do you notice when you look at:

word divided and
hyphen used

post-mortem

** _____

no hyphen

ante mortem

** _____

1238

Analyze:

post/operative
post/paralytic
post/uterine
post/axial
(You pronounce)

postoperative _____

postparalytic _____

postuterine _____

postaxial _____

167

1239

Analyze:

pre/operative   preoperative   _____
pre/paralytic   preparalytic   _____
pre/frontal   prefrontal   _____
pre/cancerous   precancerous   _____
(You pronounce)

1240

Analyze:

ante/version   anteversion   _____
ante/prostatitis   anteprostatitis   _____
ante/position   anteposition   _____
ante/location   antelocation   _____
(You pronounce)

1241

Intr/a means within. Intr/a-/abdominal means

within the abdomen   * _____.

1242

Intr/a/cellular means

within a cell   * _____.

1243

Using intra and the adjectives ven/ous, spin/al, and lumb/ar, build a word meaning:

within a vein

intravenous   _____

within the spine

intraspinal   _____

within the lumbar region

intralumbar   _____
(You pronounce)

1244

Build an adjective meaning:

within an artery

intra-arterial   _____

within the cranium

intracranial   _____

within the bladder

intracystic   _____
(You pronounce)

1245

Build an adjective meaning:

within the skin

intra/derm/al   _____

within the duodenum

intra/duoden/al   _____

within the thoracic cavity

intra/thorac/ic   _____
(You pronounce)

1246

The following chart contains information about the formation of plurals from the singular. Use it to work Frames 1247 through 1264.

TO FORM PLURALS

If the Singular Ending Is	The Plural Ending Is	
a	ae	(pronounce **ae** as **i**)
us	i	
um	a	
ma	mata	
on	a	
is	es	
ix	ices ⎤	The **word root is usually built**
ex	ices ⎬	from the plural form of words
ax	aces ⎦	ending in **ix**, **ex**, and **ax**. (e.g., radix, radic/es radic/otomy radic/i/form)

bursae
bur' si
conjunctivae
con junk ti' vi
fossae
fos' i

1247

Form the plural of:

bursa _____

conjunctiva _____

fossa _____

vertebra
ver' te bra
pleura
plu' ra
cornea
kor' nea

1248

Give the singular of:

vertebrae _____

pleurae _____

corneae _____

bacilli
ba sil' i
bronchi
bron' ki
cocci
kok' si

1249

Form the plural of:

bacillus _____

bronchus _____

coccus _____

focus
fo' kus
locus
lo' kus
nucleus
noo kli' us

1250

Give the singular of:

foci _____

loci _____

nuclei _____

169

atria
a' tria
deliria
de lir' e a
ilea
(You pronounce)

1251

Form the plural of:

atrium   _____

delirium   _____

ileum   _____

1252

Give the singular of:

datum
bacterium
ovum
(You pronounce)

data   _____

bacteria   _____

ova   _____

carcinomata
kar sin o' ma ta
fibromata
fi bro' ma ta
lipomata
li po' ma ta

1253

Form the plural of:

carcinoma   _____

fibroma   _____

lipoma   _____

enema
en' e ma
gumma
gum' ma
stigma
stig' ma

1254

Give the singular of:

enemata   _____

gummata   _____

stigmata   _____

ganglia
gang' li a
phenomena
fe nom' en a
protozoa
pro to zo' a

1255

Form the plural of:

ganglion   _____

phenomenon   _____

protozoon   _____

zoon
zo' on
encephalon
en sef' al on
spermatozoon
sper mat' o zo on

1256

Give the singular of:

zoa   _____

encephala   _____

spermatozoa   _____

aponeuroses
ap o nu ro' ses
diagnoses
di ag no' ses
pelves
pel' ves

1257

Form the plural of:

aponeurosis   _____

diagnosis   _____

pelvis   _____

crisis
kri' sis
naris
na' ris
prognosis
prog no' sis

1258
Give the singular of:
crises _____
nares _____
prognoses _____

appendices
cortices
thoraces
(You pronounce)

1259
Form the plural of:
appendix _____
cortex _____
thorax _____

appendic
cortic
thorac
(You pronounce)

1260
Give the word root (see information on page 169).
that usually refers to:
the appendix _____
the cortex _____
the thorax _____

appendic/o

cortic/o

thorac/o

1261
The combining form of the word roots you just dis-
covered takes the **o**. They become:
appendic _____ /
cortic _____ /
thorac _____ /

appendic/itis
ap pen di si' tis

cortic/al
kor' tic al

thorac/o/centesis
tho rak o sen te' sis

1262
With this new knowledge that you found for yourself, build a word meaning:
inflammation of the appendix
_____ /

pertaining to the cortex
_____ /

surgical puncture of the thorax
_____ / /

apices
fornices
varices

1263
Form the plural of:
apex _____
fornex _____
varix _____

171

1264
Form the plural of:

sarcomata
septa
radii
maxillae
(You pronounce)

    sarcoma   _____

    septum   _____

    radius   _____

    maxilla   _____

1265

free frame

There are other ways for forming plurals. These apply to only a few words. When you meet these words and have a question about how their plural forms are built, consult a medical dictionary.

1266

cervices

The cervix is the neck of the uterus. The plural of cervix is _____.

1267

cervic/o

Build the word root–combining form for cervix. The combining form takes **o**. The word root–combining form is _____ / _____.

1268
Build a word meaning:
    excision of the cervix

cervic/ectomy
ser vi sek' to mi

_____ / _____.

    inflammation of the cervix

cervic/itis
ser vi sit' is

    _____ / _____

    pertaining to the cervix

cervic/al
ser vik al

    _____ / _____

1269

free frame

Cervic/o can mean the neck as well as the neck of the uterus. In usage you are not likely to confuse them. The next frame will make the point.

1270

neck

neck

the neck of the uterus

Cervic/o/facial means pertaining to the face and _____. Cervic/o/brachial means pertaining to the arm and _____. Cervic/o/vesical means pertaining to the bladder and
      * _____.

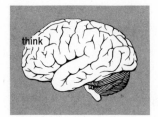

think

1271

Use the following information to work Frames 1272 through 1293. If you have forgotten a word part, remember, you may look back. If you don't know the anatomy of the respiratory system, look for a picture of it in an anatomy book. Seeing the parts as you work will make your work more interesting.

Air enters the
  nose—nas/o (Remember rhin/o? Use nas/o in
                    this work.)
goes to the
  pharynx—pharyng/o
to the
  larynx—laryng/o
to the
  trachea—trache/o
to the
  bronch/i—bronch/o
      (us)
to the
  part of the lung where it enters the bloodstream.
The lungs are covered by the
  pleura—pleur/o

1272

Nas/o/antr/itis means inflammation of the antrum
and the _____.

nose

1273

Nas/o/ment/al means pertaining to the chin and
_____.

nose

1274

Build a word meaning:

nas/al
na' zal

  pertaining to the nose _____/_____.
  inflammation of the nose

nas/itis
na zi' tis

               _____/_____.

  instrument to examine the nose

nas/o/scop/e
na' zo skop

         _____/____/_____/____.

173

1275

Build a word (you may use your dictionary if necessary) meaning:

inflammation of nose and pharynx

nas/o/pharyng/itis

_____/___/_____/_____

pertaining to the nasal and frontal bones

nas/o/front/al

_____/___/_____/_____

pertaining to the nose and lacrimal duct

nas/o/lacrim/al
(You pronounce)

_____/___/_____/_____

1276

Nas/o/pharyng/eal means pertaining to the

nose and pharynx

*_____.

1277

pharynx
far' inks

A pharyng/o/lith is a calculus in the wall of the

_____.

1278

pharynx (Work on the
pronunciation)

A pharyng/o/myc/osis is a fungus disease of the

_____.

1279

Build a word meaning:

inflammation of the pharynx

pharyngitis
far in ji' tis

_____/_____

herniation of the pharynx

pharyngocele
far in' go sel

_____/___/_____

incision of the pharynx

pharyngotomy
far in got' o mi

_____/_____

1280

Build a word meaning (you put in diagonals):

disease of the pharynx

pharyng/o/path/y
pharyng/o/plast/y
pharyng/o/scop/e

_____

surgical repair of the pharynx

(You pronounce—review
Frames 586–594)

_____

instrument to examine the pharynx

_____

1281

A laryng/o/cele is a

herniation of the larynx

**_____.

174

1282
Build a word meaning:
  any disease of the larynx

laryngopathy

_____

  instrument used to examine the larynx

laryngoscope

laryngospasm
(You pronounce)

  spasm of the larynx

_____

a condition of the trachea
with pus formation (in
your own words)

1283
Trache/o/py/osis means **_____
_____.

hemorrhage from the
trachea

1284
Trache/orrhagia means **_____
_____.

1285
Build a word meaning:
  pain in the trachea

trachealgia
tra ke al' ji a

_____ / _____

  incision into the trachea

tracheotomy
tra ke ot' o mi

_____ / _____

  herniation of the trachea

tracheocele
tra' ke o sel

_____ / ___ / _____

1286
Build a word meaning:
  examination of the trachea

tracheoscopy

_____

  pertaining to the trachea

tracheal

_____

tracheolaryngotomy
(You pronounce)

  incision of trachea and larynx

_____

inflammation of the
bronchi

1287
Bronchitis means
  *_____.

an instrument to examine
the bronchi

A bronchoscope is
  *_____.

175

1288

Build a word meaning:
  calculus in a bronchus

bronch/o/lith
bron' ko lith

_____ / _____ / _____

  examination of a bronchus (with instrument)

bronch/o/scop/y
bron kos' ko pi

_____ / _____ / _____ / _____

  bronchial hemorrhage

bronch/orrhagia
bron kor a' ji a

_____ / _____

1289

Build a word meaning:
  formation of a new opening into a bronchus

bronchostomy

  _____

  spasm of a bronchus

bronchospasm

  _____

bronchorrhaphy
(You pronounce)

  suturing of a bronchus

  _____

1290

Pleur/al means

pertaining to the pleura

  *_____.

inflammation of the
pleura

Pleur/itis means

  *_____.

1291

Build a word meaning:
  pain in the pleura

pleur/algia
plu ral' ji a
pleur/o/dynia
plu o din' i a

  _____ / _____ or

  _____ / _____ / _____

pleur/o/centesis
plu ro sen te' sis

  surgical puncturing of the pleura

  _____ / _____ / _____

1292

Build a word meaning:
  pertaining to the pleura and viscer/a

pleurovisceral

  _____

  calculus in the pleura

pleurolith

  _____

pleurectomy
(You pronounce)

  excision of part of the pleura

  _____

1293

In your dictionary the word that follows pleurectomy or pleurin is _____.

pleurisy

Read all your dictionary has to say about this disease.

1294

The word sinister means wicked or evil. The Latin word sinister means **left** or **left handed.** In medieval times when superstition was rampant, the majority of the people (who were right handed) considered left-handed people cursed by the devil. Hence these unfortunate few people became the personification of evil. This is how sinister found its common, contemporary meaning.

a little story frame

1295

In medicine you go back to the original meaning of sinister to find the word root–combining form, sinistr/o, which means _____.

left

1296

Sinistr/ad means toward the _____.

left

1297

Using sinistr/o build a word meaning:
pertaining to the left

sinistr/al
sin' is tral

_____ / _____

displacement of the heart to the left

sinistr/o/cardi/a
sin is tro kar' di a

_____ / _____ / _____ / _____

pertaining to the left half of the cerebrum

sinistr/o/cerebr/al
sin is tro ser' e bral

_____ / _____ / _____ / _____

1298

With manual and pedal, build a word meaning:
left-handed _____

sinistromanual
sinistropedal
(You pronounce)

left-footed _____

1299

The opposite of sinistr/o is dextr/o. Dextr/o means

right

_____ .

1300

Dextr/ad means toward the _____.

right

1301

Build a word meaning:
pertaining to the right

dextr/al
dex' tral

_____ / _____

displacement of the heart to the right

dextr/o/cardi/a
deks tro kar' di a

_____ / _____ / _____ / _____

displacement of the stomach to the right

dextr/o/gastr/ia
deks tro gas' tri a

_____ / _____ / _____ / _____

177

1302

Refer to frame 1298 if necessary, and build a word meaning:

right-handed

dextromanual

dextropedal
(You pronounce)

right-footed

_____

1303

Vas is a word meaning vessel, Vas/o is another word root–combining form for vessel. Vas/o/dilatation means enlarging the diameter of a

vessel

_____.

1304

Vas/o/constriction is the opposite of vas/o/dilatation. Vas/o/constriction means ** _____

decreasing the size of the
diameter of a vessel

_____.

1305

Vas/o/motor is an adjective which refers to nerves that control the tone of the blood

vessel

_____ walls.

1306

Using vas/o build a word meaning:

vasal
va' sal

pertaining to a vessel _____ / _____

vasospasm
vas' o spazm

spasm of a vessel

_____ / _____ / _____

vasotripsy
vas' o trip si

crushing of a vessel

_____ / _____ / _____

(with forceps for hemorrhage)

1307

You examine the words in
your dictionary to see what
kinds begin with vas/o.

(Skip this frame unless you are using Taber's dictionary.) Look at the words used in your dictionary beginning with vas or vas/o. Only six of them use the common medical forms and could be confused with angi/o. Three of these were used in the preceding frame. These three refer to the vas deferens only—no other vessel.

178

1308

Build a word meaning:
   incision into the vas deferens

_____/_____

   suture of the vas deferens

_____/_____

   making a new opening into the vas deferens

_____/_____

vasotomy
vas ot' o mi

vasorrhaphy
vas or' a fi

vasostomy
va zos' to mi

1309

The word root–combining form that refers to tissue is **hist/o.** A hist/o/tome is an instrument used to cut _____ for study.

tissue or tissues

1310

A substance that is hist/o/genous is a substance that is made by a _____.

tissue

1311

Build a word meaning:
   the study of tissue

_____/____/_____/_____

   one who studies tissues

_____/____/_____/_____

   a tumor composed of tissue

_____/_____

hist/o/log/y
his tol' o ge

hist/o/log/ist
his tol' o gist

hist/oma
(You pronounce)

1312

Build a word meaning:
   an embryonic tissue (cell)

_____/____/_____

   a tissue cell _____/____/_____/_____

   resembling tissue _____/_____

histoblast
histocyte
histoid
(You pronounce)

1313

Ne/o in words means new. Ne/o/genesis means regeneration of _____ tissue.

new

1314

Ne/o/nat/al refers to the _____ born. A ne/o/plasm is a tumor or _____ growth (formation—plasm/o).

new

new

179

1315

ne/o/plasm
neoplasm
ne' o plazm

Ne/o/plasm refers to any kind of tumor or new growth. A nonmalignant tumor is called a

_____ / _____ / _____ .

1316

neoplasm
neoplasm

A neoplasm may also be a malignant tumor. Carcinoma is a _____ . A melanoma is also a _____ .

1317

neoplasm

A sarcoma is also a _____ .

1318

Build a word meaning:

ne/o/cyt/e

new cell _____ / _____ / _____ / e

ne/o/path/y

any new disease _____ / _____ / _____ / y

ne/o/phob/ia
(You pronounce)

abnormal fear of new things
_____ / _____ / _____ / _____

Work Review Sheets 30 and 31.

1319

There are two combining forms that mean night. One is **noct/i.** Noct/i/luca are microscopic marine animals that make the ocean glow during the

night

_____ .

1320

Those of you who have studied music, know that a noct/urne is dreamy music, sometimes called

night

_____ music.

1321

Noct/ambulism literally means walking at night. Sleep walking is what you mean when you use the

noctambulism
nok tam' bu lizm

word_____ / _____ .

1322

Noctambulism can occur at any age, but childhood is the most common age for

noctambulism

_____ .

1323

A person is not really asleep when he sleepwalks. People appear to be asleep but are really suppressing the memory of what they do. They are indulging

noctambulism

in _____ .

1324
The other combining form for night is **nyct/o.** Nyct/algia means pain during the _____.

night

1325
Nyct/albumin/ur/ia means the presence of albumin in the urine only during the _____.

night

1326
Nyct/al/opia means night blindness or difficulty in seeing at night. Vitamin A is associated with night vision. Lack of vitamin A in the diet is one cause of _____.

nyctalopia
nik ta lo' pi a

1327
Nyct/al/opia has several causes. Retinal fatigue from exposure to very bright light is a cause of _____.

nyctalopia

1328
Retinitis pigmentosa is another cause of _____.

nyctalopia

1329
Using noct/i and nyct/o build two words that mean:
    abnormal fear of night

nyctophobia
_____ / _____ / _____

noctiphobia
_____ / _____ / _____

    unusual attraction to the night

nyctophilia
_____ / _____ / _____
noctiphilia
(You pronounce)
_____ / _____ / _____

1330
Noct/uria means excessive urination during the night. Another word that means the same thing is _____ / _____.

nycturia
nik tu' ri a

1331
Two words that mean excessive urination during the night are: .

nycturia
_____ / _____

nocturia _most often used_
_____ / _____

1332
Ankyl/o means stiff or not movable. Ankylosed means stiffened. Ankyl/o/blephar/on means adhesions resulting in

immovable eyelids
** _____.

181

1333

Ankyl/osis is a condition of

stiffness

_____ .

Use the following chart to build words through Frames 1335.

COMBINING FORM	WITH NOUN ENDING
aden/o	aden/ia
cardi/o	cardi/a
cheil/o	cheil/ia
dactyl/o	dactyl/ia
dent/o	dent/ia
derm/o	derm/a
	/ia
gastr/o	gastr/ia
gloss/o	gloss/ia
onych/o	onych/ia
ophthalm/o	ophthalm/ia
ot/o	ot/ia
phag/o	phag/ia
pneumon/o	pneumon/ia
proct/o	proct/ia
urethr/o	urethr/a

1334

Ankyl/o/stom/a means lockjaw (stiff jaw). Build a word meaning **(remember, you may look back)**:
adhesions of lips (immovable lips)

ankylocheilia

_____ / _____ / _____

closure (immobility) of the anus

ankyloproctia

_____ / _____ / _____

abnormal fear of ankylosis

ankylophobia
(You pronounce)

_____ / _____ / _____

1335

Build a word meaning:
tongue tied (stiff tongue)

ankyl/o/gloss/ia

_____ / _____ / _____

adhesions of fingers (immovable fingers)

ankyl/o/dactyl/ia

_____ / _____ / _____

1336

noun

ia is a _____ (noun/adjective/verb) ending.

1337

Do you remember the origin of o/o/phor/o (Frame 574)? O/o/phor/o refers to the organ that

bears

_____ ova.

1338

Ex/o/phor/ia refers to imbalance of the muscle that _____ the eye outward (wall eye). Es/o/phor/ia refers to imbalance of the muscle that _____ the eye mesially (cross eye).

carries or bears

carries or bears

1339

The instrument that measures the tone and pull of the eye-carrying (bearing) muscles is a

_____ / ___ / _____.

phor/o/meter
phorometer
for om' et er

1340

Hyper/phor/ia results when an eye muscle carries one eye upward. When one eye turns downward, we call it _____ / _____ / _____.

hypo/phor/ia
hypophoria
hi po for' ri a

1341

Dys/phor/ia means a feeling of depression. The patient carries with him an ill (bad) feeling. The word that means feeling of well being is

euphoria
u fo' ri a

_____ / _____.

(Refer to Frame 872 if necessary.)

1342

When a person's diet is good, he has enough rest, and the world is a wonderful place to be, he is enjoying the state of _____.

euphoria

1343

The study of people, insects, or animals that carry (bear) disease is called

phorology
fo rol' o ji

_____ / ___ / ___ / _____.

1344

Stasis is a word meaning **stopping** or **controlling**. To say that you control an organ or what that organ produces, use the combining form for the organ (or product), plus the word _____.

stasis
(You pronounce)

183

1345

A fung/i/stasis is an agent that

controls or stops

control

_____ fungus growth. Lymph/o/

stasis means _____ of lymph flow.

1346

control or stopping of
bile secretion

Chol/e/stasis means

**
_____.

(Refer to Frame 495 if necessary.)

1347

enter/o/stasis
enterostasis
en ter os' ta sis
py/o/stasis
pyostasis
pi os' ta sis

Read Frame 1345 again. Build a word meaning:
controlling the small intestine

_____ / _____ / _____

stopping the formation of pus

_____ / _____ / _____

1348

Build a word meaning:
controlling the flow of blood

hemostasis
he mos' ta sis

_____ / _____ / _____

checking flow in the veins

phlebostasis or venostasis
fleb os' ta sis

_____ / _____ / _____

checking flow in the arteries

arteriostasis
ar te ri os' ta sis

_____ / _____ / _____

1349

Schiz/o, schist/o, and schis/o are all combining
forms that have a complicated evolution from
Greek. They mean split (cleft or fissure). Analyze
the following words:

schiz/o/phren/ia
skiz o fre' ni a
schiz/o/phas/ia
schiz/o/cyt/e

    schizophrenia _____

    schizophasia _____

    schizocyte _____

1350

Analyze the following words:

schist/o/gloss/ia
skis to glos' i a
schist/o/cyt/e
schist/o/thorax

    schistoglossia _____

    schistocyte _____

    schistothorax _____

palat/o/schis/is
pal a tos' kis is
uran/o/schis/is
u ran os' kis is
rach/i/schis/is
ra kis' kis is

1351

Analyze the following words:

    palatoschisis _____

    uranoschisis _____

    rachischisis _____

1352

In your dictionary, read about the disease schisto-somiasis and schistosoma. Schistosomiasis is a very important disease in terms of world health. Because of increased worldwide travel all people should be concerned with the disease,

schistosomiasis

_____ / / _____ / _____ .

organism in water that causes disease

mejico

1353

Learn the words involving the combining forms for "split" that you need to know. Surely schizophrenia will be one of them. Use your dictionary to understand the words you (or your teacher) decide you should learn. Schiz/o, schist/o, and schis/o mean

split

_____ .

Use the labels on the following drawing plus your dictionary to work Frames 1354 through 1391.

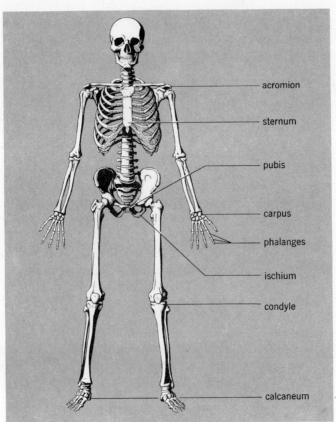

— acromion

— sternum

— pubis

— carpus

— phalanges

— ischium

— condyle

— calcaneum   *heel*

calcanea kal ka' ni a (if necessary, refer back to Frame 1246)	**1354** Locate the calcaneum. The plural of calcaneum is _____ .
calcane	**1355** From calcaneum and calcanea, derive the word root for the heel. _____
	1356 In your medical dictionary, look at the words be- ginning with calcane. Derive the combining form that is used in words that refer to the heel.
calcane/o	_____ / ___

calcane/al
calcaneal
kal ka' neal
calcane/o/dynia
calcaneodynia
kal ka ne o din' ia
	1357
	Close your dictionary. Now build a word meaning:
	    pertaining to the heel
	                      _____ / _____
	    pain in the heel
	   _____ / ___ / _____

heel	**1358** Calcane/o in a word refers to the _____ .
carpi	**1359** Locate the carpus. The plural of carpus is _____ .
carp	**1360** From carpus and carpi, derive a word root that refers to the wrist. It is _____ .
carp/o	**1361** Look at the words (in your medical dictionary) that begin with carp. The combining form that is used in words about the wrist is _____ / ___ .

carpal
kar' pal
 	
carpoptosis
kar pop to' sis
 	
carpectomy
kar pek' to mi
	1362
	Close your dictionary. Build a word meaning:
	    pertaining to the wrist (adjective)
	                      _____ / _____
	    prolapse of the wrist
	         _____ / ___ / _____
	    excision of all or part of the wrist
	               _____ / _____

wrist	**1363** Carp/o in a word refers to the _____ .

1364

You are now finding your own word root-combining forms. Feels good, doesn't it? Let's do some more.

congratulations!

1365

Locate the ischium. The plural of ischium is

ischia

_____ .

1366

From ischium and ischia, derive a word root that refers to the part of the hip bone on which the body rests when sitting. The word root is

ischi

_____ .

1367

Look up words that begin with ischi. The combining form that is used in words to refer to the ischium is

ischi/o

_____/_____ .

1368

In your dictionary, find a word meaning:

pertaining to the ischium and rectum

ischiorectal
is ki o rek' tal

_____/_____/_____/_____

neuralgic pain in the hip (synonym is sciatica)

ischioneuralgia
is ki o nu ral' ji a

_____/_____/_____/_____

pertaining to the ischium and pubis

ischiopubic
is ki o pu' bic

_____/_____/_____/_____

1369

Close your dictionary. Build a word meaning:

pertaining to the ischium

ischial
is' ki al

_____/_____

herniation through the ischium

ischiocele
is' ki o sel

_____/_____/_____

1370

Ischi/o in a word refers to the part of the hip bone known as the _____ .

ischium
is' ki um

1371

Locate the pubis. The plural of pubis is

pubes
pu' bes

_____ .

1372

The word root-combining form used in words about the pubis is _____/_____ . (Don't forget your dictionary.)

pub/o (used most often)
or
pubi/o

1373

Close your dictionary. Using pub/o, build a word meaning:

pubic
pu' bik

pubofemoral
pu bo fem' or al

pertaining to the pubis _____/_____

pertaining to the femur and pubis

_____/____/_____/_____

1374

pubis

Pub/o in a word refers to the _____.

1375

Locate the sternum. The word root–combining form

stern/o

for sternum is _____/____.

1376

You did that one all alone! With your dictionary still open, find a word meaning:

pertaining to the sternum and pericardium

sternopericardial

sternocostal
(You pronounce)

_____

pertaining to the sternum and ribs

_____

1377

Close the dictionary. Build a word meaning:

pertaining to the sternum

sternal

_____/_____

pain in the sternum

sternalgia
sternodynia
(You pronounce)

_____/_____ or

_____/____/_____

1378

sternum
breastbone

Stern/o in a word makes you think of the _____ which is the

_____.

1379

bones of the fingers
and toes (can omit
fingers or toes)

Locate the phalanges. They are the ** _____

_____.

1380

The word root for phalanges is

phalang

_____.

1381
Build a word meaning:
   inflammation of phalanges

_____ / _____

   excision of one or more phalanges

_____ / _____

phalang/itis
fa lan ji' tis

phalang/ectomy
fa lan jek' to mi

1382
Locate the acromion. It is a projection of the

_____ (dictionary if necessary).

scapula

1383
The word root–combining form for the acromion is

_____ / _____.

acromi/o

1384
Find a word in your dictionary meaning:
   pertaining to the acromion

_____ / _____

   pertaining to the acromion and humerus

_____ / _____ / _____ / _____

acromial
ak ro' mi al
acromi/o/humer/al
acromiohumeral
a kro' mi o hu mer al

1385
Look at Frame 1384. Can it start you looking for another word root–combining form? Try. It is

_____ / _____.

humer/o

1386
Humer/o is used in words to refer to the bone of the upper arm, which is named the

_____.

humerus

1387
Find three words in your dictionary that begin with humer or humer/o. They are:

_____

_____

_____

(pick three out of four)

humeral
humeroradial
humeroscapular
humeroulnar

1388
Could Frame 1387 start you building other word root–combining forms? Well, it isn't necessary, but you may if you like.

It could get to be
a never-ending thing,
couldn't it?

189

1389

Refer back to the drawing of the skeleton. Locate a condyle. A condyle is a rounded process that occurs on many bones. The word root for condyle

condyl   is _____ .

1390

Build a word meaning:

   excision of a condyle

condylectomy
kon di lek' to mi   _____ / _____

condyloid   resembling a condyle
kon' di loid
                         _____ / _____

epicondyle   above a condyle
ep i kon' dil   epi / _____

1391

Condyl/ar is an adjective meaning pertaining to a

condyle   _____ .

1392

The plural of ganglion is ganglia. A ganglion is a collection of nerve cell bodies. Now that you have a system, form the word root–combining form for

gangli/o   ganglion. _____ / _____

1393

Practice using the singulars and plurals correctly by working Frames 1393 through 1397. The singular

ganglion   noun built from gangli/o is
gang' li on

                               _____ .

1394

ganglia   The plural form of the noun built from gangli/o is
gang' li a
                         _____ .

1395

There **is** a mass of gray matter beneath the third ventricle called the basal optic

ganglion   _____ .

1396

The main cerebral nerve centers are called the
ganglia   cerebral _____ .

1397

Any one of three neural masses found in the cervi-
ganglion   cal region is called a cervical _____ ,
                         whereas all three are referred to as the cervical
ganglia   _____ .

1398

Thromb/o is the word root–combining form that means clot. Thromb/o/angi/itis means inflammation of a vessel with formation of a

clot

_____.

1399

excision of a
thrombus (clot).

Thromb/ectomy means ** _____

_____.

1400

The proper medical way to say clot is to say thrombus. A synonym for clot is

thrombus

_____.

inflammation of a lymph
vessel with formation
of a thrombus (clot) or
a condition of this

1401

Thromb/o/lymph/angi/itis means ** _____

_____

_____.

inflammation of a
vein with thrombus
formation

1402

Thromb/o/phleb/itis means ** _____

_____

_____.

1403

Using thromb/o, build a word meaning:
   a condition of forming a thrombus

thrombosis
throm bo' sis

_____/_____

   a cell that aids clotting

thrombocyte
throm' bo sit

_____/_____/_____/_____

thromboid
throm boyd'

   resembling a thrombus

_____/_____

1404

Build a word meaning:
   formation of a thrombus

thrombogenesis
throm' bo jen es is

_____/_____/_____

   destruction of a thrombus

thrombolysis
throm bol' i sis

_____/_____/_____

   lack of cells that aid clotting

thrombocytopenia
throm bo si to pe' ni a

_____/_____/_____/_____/_____

1405

Trich/o is used in words to mean hair. A trich/o/genous substance promotes the growth of

hair

_____.

191

hair

1406
Lith/iasis is the formation of calculi (in the wrong place). Trich/iasis is the formation of _____ (in the wrong places).

1407
Using trich/o, build a word meaning:
  hairy heart (noun)

trichocardia
trik o kar' di a

_____ / ____ / _____ / _____

  hairy tongue (noun)

trichoglossia
trik o glos' si a

_____ / ____ / _____ / _____

  resembling hair

trichoid

_____ / _____

  abnormal fear of hair

trichophobia

_____ / ____ / _____ / _____

  any hair disease

trichopathy

_____ / ____ / _____ / _____

eat

1408
Phag/o means _____ . (You may refer to Frame 508 if necessary.)

eats (or ingests)

1409
A phag/o/cyt/e is a cell that _____ micro-organisms. Phag/o/cyt/osis is the process of the

eating (or ingesting)

cells _____ micro-organisms.

1410
A large phagocyte is called a macr/o/phag/e. A small phagocyte is called a

micr/o/phag/e
microphage
mi' kro faj

_____ / ____ / _____ / _____ .

1411
Onych/o/phag/y is nail biting. A word that means hair swallowing is

trich/o/phag/y
trik of' a ji

_____ / ____ / _____ / _____ .

Air swallowing is

aer/o/phag/y
a er of' a ji

_____ / ____ / _____ / _____ .

Work Review Sheets 32 and 33.

Use the following partially labeled drawings of the eye plus your dictionary to work the next 41 frames.

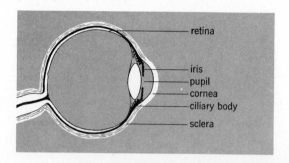

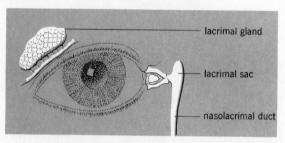

1412
Look up cornea in your dictionary. Look at the words in your dictionary that begin with **corne**. A word root–combining form for cornea is

corne/o
_____ / ___.

1413
While thinking of the meaning, analyze:

corne/itis
kor ni i' tis

corneitis _____ / _____

corne/o/ir/itis
kor ne o i ri' tis

corneoiritis
_____ / ___ / ___ / ___

corne/o/scler/a
kor ne o skle' ra

corneosclera
_____ / ___ / ___ / ___

1414
From the preceding frame find two other word roots that match labels on your drawing. They are

ir
scler
_____ and _____.

1415
Look up the first word in your dictionary beginning

sclera
skle' ra

with scler. It is _____.

1416

Read what the sclera is. Does the word root plus the meaning of the Greek word from which it is derived suggest an already familiar combining form to you? It is _____/_____, which means _____.

scler/o
hard

1417

The sclera of the eye is the "hard" outer coat of the eye. Build a word meaning:

pertaining to the sclera (adjective)

_____/_____

scler/al
skle' ral

excision of the sclera (or part)

_____/_____

scler/ectomy
skle rek' to mi

formation of an opening into the sclera

_____/_____

scler/ostomy
skle ros' to mi

1418

Go back to the other word root you found in Frame 1414. With it in mind, find the part of the eye (on your drawing) to which it refers. This is the

_____.

iris
i' ris

1419

information frame

Look up "iris" in your dictionary. **Ir** is one word root for the iris. It is very limited in use. It is always used to express inflammation, so you can see it is important if limited in use.

1420

With the information in Frame 1419 and the word root you found, build a word meaning:

inflammation of the iris

_____/_____

iritis

inflammation of the cornea and iris

_____/____/_____

corneoiritis

inflammation of the sclera and iris

_____/____/_____

scleroiritis
(You pronounce)

1421

Return to your dictionary and the word **iris.** By using the plural of iris, or by looking under the section that starts **see,** find another word root for iris. It is _____.

irid

1422

With your dictionary, find the combining form for

irid. It is _____/_____ .

irid/o

1423

Using irid/o build a word meaning:

iridocele
i rid' o sel

    herniation of the iris

_____/____/_____

iridalgia
ir id al' ji a

    pain in the iris

_____/_____

iridectomy
ir id ek' to mi

    excision of part of the iris

_____/_____

1424

Build a word meaning (you insert the diagonals):

    prolapse of the iris

irid/o/ptosis

    _____

irid/o/malac/ia

    softening of the iris

    _____

irid/orrhexis
(You pronounce)

    rupture of the iris

    _____

1425

There are two words to express paralysis of the iris.

iridoplegia

They are _____/____/_____/_____

iridoparalysis
(You pronounce)

and

_____/____/_____ .

1426

The following forms make you think of:

iris   ir _____

iris   irid/o _____

sclera (hard)   scler/o _____

cornea   corne/o _____

1427

Look up **retina** in your dictionary. Read about the retina. Look at the words beginning with retin in your dictionary. The word root–combining form for words about the retina is

retin/o

_____/_____ .

1428
Build a word meaning:
   pertaining to the retina

retinal
ret' in al

_____ / _____

   inflammation of the retina

retinitis
ret in i' tis

_____ / _____

   resembling the retina

retinoid
ret' in oyd

_____ / _____

1429
The instrument used to examine the retina is the

retinoscope
ret' in o skop

_____ / _____ / _____ / _____. The

process of examining the retina is

retinoscopy
ret in os' ko pi

_____ / _____ / _____ / _____.

1430
Look up **pupil** in your medical dictionary. Read about it. In the list of words about the pupil, find **cor**ectasis, **cor**encleisis, and iso**cor**ial. From these words, find a word root for pupil. It is _____.

cor

1431
The combining form for pupil is cor/e. Build a word meaning:
   pupil misplaced

corectopia
kor ek to' pi a
corelysis
ko rel' i sis
corectas/ia
      /is
kor ek ta' zi a

_____ / _____

   destruction of the pupil

_____ / _____ / _____ / _____

   dilatation (stretching) of the pupil

_____ / _____ / _____

1432
Cor/e/o is also used as a combining form for pupil. Using core/o, build a word meaning:
   instrument for measuring the pupil

coreometer

_____

   measurement of the pupil

coreometry

_____

coreoplasty
(You pronounce)

   plastic surgery of the pupil

_____

1433
Whether cor/e or cor/e/o is used, the word root for pupil of the eye is _____.

cor

1434

(Skip this frame unless you are using Taber's dictionary.) Go back to **cornea** in your dictionary. Under **corne, words pertaining to,** find two word roots for cornea. They are _____ and

_____ .

cera and kerat

1435

Check words beginning with **cera** and words beginning with **kerat.** The word root–combining form **most often** used to refer to the cornea is

_____ / _____ .

kerat/o

1436

Using kerat/o build a word meaning:

dilatation of the cornea

_____ / _____

keratectasia (is)
ker a tek ta' si a

herniation through the cornea

_____ / _____ / _____

keratocele
ker at' o sel

plastic operation of the cornea (corneal transplant)

_____ / _____ / _____

keratoplasty
ker' a to plas ti

1437

Build a word meaning:

incision of the cornea

_____ / _____

keratotomy

corneal rupture

_____ / _____

keratorrhexis

inflammation of cornea and sclera

_____ / _____ / _____

keratoscleritis
(You pronounce)

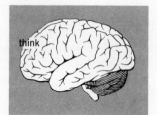

1438

The word root–combining form for **ciliary body** is **cycl/o.** Look up the ciliary body in your dictionary or an anatomy book and understand what it is.

197

1439

Turn to cycl/o words in your dictionary. Find a word meaning:

paralysis of the ciliary body (noun)

_____ / ___ / _____ / _____

paralysis of the ciliary body (adjective)

_____ / ___ / _____ / _____

cycl/o/pleg/ia
si klo ple' ji a

cycl/o/pleg/ic
si klo ple' jik

1440

Cycloplegia and cycloplegic are words used often in the practice of ophthalmology. For that reason write them both several times.

cycloplegia   *cycloplegic*

_____   _____

_____   _____

Good work—now,
remember them

1441

The following forms make you think of:

retin/o   _____

cor/e   _____

cor/e/o   _____

kerat/o   _____

cycl/o   _____

retina
pupil
pupil
cornea
ciliary body

1442

Look at the drawing of the lacrimal apparatus. The word root that you see immediately is

_____.

lacrim

1443

Look up lacrim/al in your dictionary. Lacrimal is a word that means pertaining to _____.

tears

1444

The gland which secretes tears is the

_____ gland.

lacrimal
lak' rim al

1445

The sac which collects lacrimal fluid is the

_____ sac.

lacrimal

1446

Lacrimal fluid is drained away by means of the

_____ / ___ / _____ / _____ duct.

nasolacrimal
na zo lak' rim al

198

1447

Lacrimal fluid keeps the surface of the eye moistened. It is continually forming and being removed. When there is more formed than can be removed by the apparatus, you say the person is

crying or
tearing

_____.

1448

Lacrimation means crying. Excessive crying is called **dacry**orrhea. This word gives you another word root for **tear.** It is _____.

dacry

1449

Look up words beginning with dacry in your medical dictionary. The combining form of the word root

dacry/o

dacry is _____ / _____.

1450

Analyze (you draw the diagonals):

dacry/o/cyst/itis
dak ri o sis ti' tis
dacry/o/aden/algia
dak ri o ad en al' gia
dacry/oma
dak ri o' ma

dacryocystitis _____

dacryoadenalgia _____

dacryoma _____

1451

Analyze:

dacryopyorrhea _____

dacry/o/py/orrhea

dacry/o/cyst/o/cele
dacry/o/lith
(You pronounce)

dacryocystocele _____

dacryolith _____

1452

If necessary you may use your dictionary to answer the following:

Dacryorrhea means
　　　　＊＊
_____.

excessive flow of tears
prolapse of the tear sac
instrument for cutting
　tear sac
(your own words, of
　course)

Dacryocystoptosis means
　　　　　＊＊
_____.

A dacryocystotome is
　　　　＊＊
_____.

1453

If a dacry/o/cyst/o/tome is an instrument for incising the tear sac, build a word meaning instrument for incising the:

keratotome
ker at' o tom
sclerotome
skler' o tom
cystotome
histotome
osteotome

cornea	_____
sclera	_____
bladder	_____
tissue	_____
bone	_____

1454

Build a word meaning an instrument to incise the following:

cartilage

chondrotome

_____

lithotome
myotome
neurotome
(You pronounce)

stone or calculus

_____

muscle _____

nerve _____

1455

The two combining forms used in building the word

phag/o and cyt/o

phagocyte are _____/_____ and

_____/_____ .

1456

The word phag/o/cyt/e makes you think literally

eats (or ingests)

of a cell that _____ .

1457

A phagocyte ingests (absorbs, eats—after a fashion) other cells, bacteria, or waste matter. A phago-cytoblast is an **_____

embryonic phagocyte
or a cell that will
become a phagocyte

_____ .

1458

Phagocytosis is the condition of absorption or

phagocytes

digestion by _____ .

the ingestion
(destruction or
eating) of cells by
phagocytes

1459

Cyt/o/phag/o/cyt/osis is **_____

_____ .

1460

the ingestion of
cells by phagocytes

Cyt/o/phag/y is another way of saying **_____

_____

_____ .

200

1461

An instrument for measuring cells is a

_____ / ____ / _____ . The process of

measuring cells is _____ / ____ / _____ .

cytometer
si tom' et er
cytometry
si tom' et ry

1462

Stopping or controlling cells is called

_____ / ____ / _____ . Examination

of cells is _____ / ____ / _____ / _____ .

cytostasis
si tos' to sis
cytoscopy
si tos' kop i

1463

The next five frames will give you more practice in finding word root-combining forms. (Many new words enter the medical vocabulary every day.) Refer to these next five frames to work the material in Frames 1469 through 1478.

1464

Look up **tympanum** in your dictionary. The tympanum is the _____ . The word root-combining form for tympanum is

_____ / _____ .

eardrum

tympan/o

1465

Look up **vesica**, vesicle. They mean

_____ . Their word root-combin-

ing form is _____ / _____ .

bladder

vesic/o

1466

Look up **ren** (renes). They mean

_____ . Their word root-combining

form is _____ / _____ .

kidney

ren/o

1467

Look up **podalgia**. Podalgia means pain in the

_____ . The new word root-combining form

is _____ / _____ .

foot

pod/o

1468

Look up **chirapsia**. The "literal" Greek meaning is

* _____ .

The word root-combining form for hand is

_____ / _____ .

a touching
with the hands ⊢

chir/o

201

tympan/ic
    /al
tim pan' ik

tympanotomy
tim pan ot' o mi

tympanectomy
tim pan ek' to mi

tympanites or
tympanism
(note **es** ending in
tympanites)

renal
re' nal
renopathy
ren op' ath i
ren/o/graph
    /gram
(You pronounce)

pertaining to the
kidney and intestine

pertaining to the
kidney and stomach

vesical
ves' ik al

vesicocele
ves' ik o sel

vesicoclysis
ves ik ok' lis is

podalgia or

pododynia

podogram

1469
Build a word meaning:
    pertaining to the eardrum

_____ / _____

    incision into the eardrum

_____ / _____

    excision of the eardrum

_____ / _____

1470
In your dictionary find a word that means **distended with gas**—as tight as a drum. It is

_____ .

1471
Build a word meaning:
    pertaining to the kidney

_____ / _____

    any kidney disease

_____ / _____ / _____ / _____

    record from x-ray of the kidney

_____ / _____ / _____

1472
Renointestinal means
   ** _____ .

Renogastric means
   ** _____ .

1473
Build a word meaning:
    pertaining to the bladder

_____ / _____

    herniation of a bladder

_____ / _____

    irrigation (washing) of a bladder

_____ / _____ / _____ / _____

1474
Build a word meaning:
    foot pain   _____ / _____ or

    _____ / _____ / _____

    footprint _____ / _____ / gram

1475

foot

Pod in a word makes you think of _____ .

1476

foot

In chir/o/pod/ist, pod makes you think of

_____ .

1477

hands

Chir/o in the word chiropodist means

pronounced k

_____ .

1478

Build a word meaning:

chiromegaly
ki ro meg' a li

enlargement of the hands

_____ / ___ / _____ / ___

chiroplasty
ki' ro plas ti

plastic surgery of the hands

_____ / ___ / _____ / ___

chiropody
ki rop' od i

the specialty of treating the hands and feet

_____ / ___ / _____ / ___

1479

To understand and recognize suffixes, use the following chart to work Frames 1480 through 1496.

NOUN SUFFIXES	ORDINARY EXAMPLES
ism—condition, state, or theory	commun**ism**
tion—condition or action	stimula**tion** satisfac**tion**
ist ⎱ er ⎰ —one who ity—quality	commun**ist** promp**ter** read**ability**
ADJECTIVAL SUFFIXES	
ous—condition, material	pi**ous** por**ous**
able ⎱ ible ⎰ —ability	read**able** ed**ible**

1480

condition or state

Crypt/orchid/ism is the _____ of having undescended testes.

1481

condition or state

Hyper/thyroid/ism is a _____ of too much secretion by the thyroid gland. Iso/dactyl/

condition or state

ism is a _____ involving fingers of equal length.

1482

Darwin/ism presents a theory of development.

theory

Mendel/ism presents a _____ of heredity.

1483

noun

Hypo/pituitar/ism is a _____ (noun/adjective).

1484

action

Contraction is the _____ of shortening muscles.

1485

condition

Relaxation is a _____ of diminished tension.

1486

nouns

Contraction and relaxation are _____.
(nouns/adjectives)

1487

one who

A psychiatrist is * _____ practices psychiatry. A medical practitioner is

one who

* _____ practices medicine.

1488

noun

The word practitioner is a _____.
(noun/adjective)

1489

quality

Conductivity expresses the _____ of nervous tissue related to transferring impulses.

quality

Sensitivity expresses the _____ of nervous tissue related to receiving stimuli.

1490

noun

Irritability is a _____.
(noun/adjective)

1491

material

Mucous refers to the nature of a _____

material

secreted by the mucous membrane. Serous refers to the nature of the _____ lining body cavities.

1492

condition

Nervous refers to the _____ of being under too much tension.

1493

adjectives

Words ending in **ous** are _____.
(nouns/adjectives)

1494

ability
ability

To say a food is digestible is to say it has the _____ to be digested. To say a fracture is reducible is to say that it has the _____ to be set.

1495

ability

To say that lungs are inflatable is to say that they have the _____ to inflate.

1496

adjectives

Words ending in **ible** or **able** are _____.
(nouns/adjectives)

1497

emia is a suffix that you have used without a formal introduction. If you understand emia thoroughly (which will show by your answer in Frame 1498, you may skip Frames 1499 through 1501.

1498

condition of blood
or blood condition

emia is a suffix that means *_____
_____.

1499

leuk/emia
leukemia
lu ke' mi a

Isch/emia is a condition in which blood is drained from one place. Blood cancer (too many leuk/o/cytes in the blood) is called

_____ / _____.

205

1500
Build a word meaning:
  without (not enough) blood

_____/_____

  too much blood (in one part)

_____/_____

  urine constituents in blood

_____/_____

anemia
an e' mi a

hyperemia
hi per e' mi a

uremia
u re' mi a

1501
Analyze:
  xanthemia

_____

  chloremia

_____

  erythremia

_____

xanth/emia
zan the' mi a

chlor/emia
klo re' mi a

erythr/emia
e rith e' mi a

1502
(Skip this frame unless you are using Taber's dictionary.) You are now ready to find word roots and their combining forms by another method. Look up the word spine in your dictionary. A synonym for spine is _____.

backbone

1503
(Skip this frame unless you are using Taber's dictionary.) Look at the words listed under "RS" (related subject). The word root given for you to look up is _____ words.

rach

1504
Look at the words beginning with **rach**. There are two combining forms given. They are
_____/_____ and _____/_____.

rach/i and
rachi/o

1505
Words beginning with rachi/o refer to the
_____.

spine

1506
Using rachi/o, build a word meaning:
  spine pain

_____/_____

  incision into the spine

_____/_____

rachialgia
ra ki al' ji a

rachiotomy
ra ki ot' o mi

206

1507
Using rachi/o, build a word meaning:
a synonym for rachialgia

_____ / _____ / _____

instrument to measure spinal curvature

_____ / _____ / _____ / _____

spinal paralysis

_____ / _____ / _____ / _____

rachiodynia
ra ki o din' i a

rachiometer
ka ki om' et er

rachioplegia
ra ki o ple' ji a

1508
In the same manner using rach/i, build a word meaning:
fissure of the spine (split spine)

_____ / _____ / _____ / is

inflammation of the spine

_____ / _____

rach/i/schis/is
ra kis' kis is

rach/itis
(You pronounce)

1509
Words beginning with rach/i or rachi/o refer to the _____ .

spine

1510
To find a word root for the **navel,** look up navel in the dictionary. A synonym for navel is

_____ .

umbilicus

1511
(Skip this frame unless you are using Taber's dictionary.) There are not many "RS" words for navel so look up its synonym, "umbilicus." The RS words for umbilicus send you to _____ words.

omphal

1512
Turn to words beginning with omphal. The combining form for omphal is _____ / _____ .

omphal/o

1513
Words beginning with omphal/o refer to the

_____ .

navel or umbilicus

207

1514

Using omphal/o, build a word meaning:
pertaining to the navel

omphalic
om fal' ik

_____ / _____

omphalectomy
om fal ek' to mi

excision of the umbilicus

_____ / _____

omphalocele
om fal' o sel

herniation of the navel

_____ / _____ / _____

1515

Build a word meaning:
umbilical hemorrhage

omphalorrhagia

_____ / _____

discharge flowing from the navel

omphalorrhea

_____ / _____

omphalorrhexis
(You pronounce)

rupture of the navel

_____ / _____

1516

navel

Words containing omphal/o refer to the _____,
which is also called the

umbilicus

_____ .

1517

Find a word root for **nail** by looking in your dictionary at the section **nail**–nail biting. It is

onych *onie*

_____ .

1518

By studying words beginning with onych, you can
find its combining form. The word root–combining

onych/o

form that refers to **nail** is _____ / _____ .

1519

Build a word meaning:
resembling a finger nail

onychoid
on' i koyd

_____ / _____

tumor of the nail (or nail bed)

onychoma
on i ko' ma

_____ / _____

any nail condition

onychosis
on i ko' sis

_____ / _____

1520
Build a word meaning:
   softening of the nails

onychomalacia
_____ / _____ / _____ / _____

   fungus infection (condition) of the nails

onychomycosis
_____ / _____ / _____ / _____

onychophagy
(You pronounce)
   nail biting (eating)
_____ / _____ / _____ / _____

hidden nail or
condition of nail
being hidden

1521
Onych/o/crypt/osis means literally ** _____
_____ .

1522
Look up onychocryptosis in your dictionary. It refers to an

ingrown toenail
   * _____ .

1523
(Skip this frame unless you are using Taber's dictionary.) A word root–combining form for the dia-

phren/o
(diaphragm/o)
phragm is _____ / _____ .

1524
When you look up **phren/o** or **phren/o** words, you
find it can also be used to refer to the

mind
   _____ .

1525
Phot/o is used in words to refer to

light
   _____ .

1526
Pharmac/o is used in words to refer to

drugs or medicine
   _____ .

1527
(Skip this frame unless you are using Taber's dic-
om
tionary.) A good word root for shoulder is _____ .

om/o
Its combining form is _____ / _____ .

1528
(Skip this frame unless you are using Taber's dictionary.) In addition to **muc,** a word root that refers

myx
to mucus is _____ . Its combining form is

myx/o
_____ / _____ .

1529
see introduction
You now know a good system for word building.

1530

Frames 1260 to 1262 and 1354 to 1375

You know many prefixes, suffixes, and combining forms. You even know how to find word root-combining forms from singular and plural forms of a word.

1531

intermittently for the last 167 frames

You also know several ways to find combining forms in your dictionary.

Work Review Sheets 34 and 35.

1532

To prove it again, look up trauma in your dictionary. It means a

a wound or injury

* _____.

1533

Look at the next several words following trauma. The combining form for trauma is

traumat/o

_____ / ____.

1534

traumat/o/log/y
traw ma tol' o ji

The study of caring for wounds is called

_____ / ____ / _____ / ____.

relax

1535

See, you really are competent in systematic Medical Terminology.

APPENDIX A

Review Sheets

REVIEW SHEET NO. 1

Following are a series of review sheets. Whenever a form is beginning to fade in your memory, you should rework the previous review sheets. Work them often. Cover the right column with a piece of paper and move it down as you do each word part.

WORD PART	MEANING	
acr/o	_____	extremity
megal/o	_____	enlargement
dermat/o	_____	skin
cyan/o	_____	blue
derm/o	_____	skin
leuk/o	_____	white
penia	_____	lack of
cardi/o	_____	heart
gastr/o	_____	stomach
cyt/o	_____	cell
mania	_____	madness
algia	_____	pain
ectomy	_____	excision
otomy	_____	incision
ostomy	_____	new opening
duoden/o	_____	duodenum
electr/o	_____	electricity
hyper	_____	more than normal
hypo	_____	less than normal
emesis	_____	vomiting
troph/o	_____	development
aden/o	_____	gland
path/o	_____	disease
lip/o	_____	fat

213

REVIEW SHEET NO. 2

Cover the right column with a sheet of paper and move it down as you finish each word part.

MEANING	WORD PART	
fat	_____	lip/o
more than normal	_____	hyper
madness	_____	mania
enlargement	_____	megal/o
electricity	_____	electr/o
white	_____	leuk/o
development	_____	troph/o
incision	_____	**ot**omy
blue	_____	cyan/o
disease	_____	path/o
stomach	_____	gastr/o
extremity	_____	acr/o
vomiting	_____	emesis
new opening	_____	**os**tomy
skin	_____	dermat/o–derm/o
skin	_____	derm/o–dermat/o
gland	_____	aden/o
heart	_____	cardi/o
less than normal	_____	hypo
excision	_____	**ec**tomy
lack of	_____	penia
duodenum	_____	duoden/o
pain	_____	algia
cell	_____	cyt/o

REVIEW SHEET NO. 3

Cover the right column with a sheet of paper and move it down as you finish each word part.

WORD PART	MEANING	
carcin/o	_____	cancer
malac/o	_____	softening
muc/o	_____	mucus
laryng/o	_____	larynx
cephal/o	_____	head
dyn/ia	_____	pain
cele	_____	herniation
oste/o	_____	bone
arthr/o	_____	joint
chondr/o	_____	cartilage
cost/o	_____	rib
inter	_____	between
dent/o	_____	tooth
ab	_____	from
ad	_____	toward
abdomin/o	_____	abdomen
cyst/o	_____	bladder
centesis	_____	puncture
thorac/o	_____	thorax or chest
plast/o, plast/y	_____	repair
hydr/o	_____	water
therap/o	_____	treatment
pub/o	_____	pubis
metr/o, meter	_____	measure
pelv/i	_____	pelvis

REVIEW SHEET NO. 4

MEANING	WORD PART	
rib	_____	cost/o
larynx	_____	laryng/o
pubis	_____	pub/o
cancer	_____	carcin/o
repair	_____	plast/o /y
tooth	_____	dent/o
mucus	_____	muc/o
from	_____	ab
pelvis	_____	pelv/i
herniation	_____	cele
softening	_____	malac/o
water	_____	hydr/o
abdomen	_____	abdomin/o
bone	_____	oste/o
puncture	_____	centesis
measure	_____	metr/o, meter
head	_____	cephal/o
joint	_____	arthr/o
between	_____	inter
treatment	_____	therap/o
thorax or chest	_____	thorac/o
bladder	_____	cyst/o
toward	_____	ad
cartilage	_____	chondr/o
pain	_____	dyn/ia

Should you rework Review Sheets 1 and 2?

REVIEW SHEET NO. 5

Suffixes that make a word an adjective meaning pertaining to:

SUFFIXES	EXAMPLE
al	duoden/al
ic	gastr/ic
ar	palm/ar
ac	cardi/ac

Prepare a list of word roots taking **al** and word roots taking **ic** to make them adjectives. Add to this list as you progress through your course.

al	ic	ar	ac
costal	cephalodynic	lumbar	cardiac
chondrocostal	abdominal		thorac
dental	abdomenocystic		
abdomenal	hydrocephalic		
spinal			
cerebrospinal			
supercranial			
craniocerebral			

REVIEW SHEET NO. 6

WORD PART	MEANING	
supra	_____	above
crani/o	_____	cranium (skull)
cerebr/o	_____	cerebrum
mening/o	_____	meninges
staphyl/o	_____	uvula or staphylococcus
cocc/o	_____	coccus
py/o	_____	pus
gen/o gen/ic	_____	⎰ generation
gen/esis	_____	⎱ origin
gen/ous	_____	beginning
orrhea	_____	flow
ot/o	_____	ear
rhin/o	_____	nose
lith/o	_____	stone or calculus
chol/e	_____	gall—bile
brad/y	_____	slow
phag/o /ia	_____	eat
kinesi/o	_____	movement
log/o logy logist	_____	study
malac/o	_____	softening
tach/y	_____	fast
pne/o	_____	breathe
a	_____	without
dys	_____	bad, painful, difficult
peps/ia	_____	digestion
cyst/o	_____	bladder
strept/o	_____	twisted

223

REVIEW SHEET NO. 7

MEANING	WORD PART	
flow	_____	orrhea
slow	_____	brad/y
digestion	_____	peps/ia
twisted	_____	strept/o
gall–bile	_____	chol/e
nose	_____	rhin/o
cerebrum	_____	cerebr/o
pus	_____	py/o
movement	_____	kinesi/o
fast	_____	tach/y
meninges	_____	mening/o
{beginning	_____	gen/ous—gen/o
origin	_____	gen/esis
generation	_____	gen/ic
bad, painful, difficult	_____	dys
above	_____	supra
coccus	_____	cocc/o
without	_____	a
study	_____	log/o—logy—logist
stone or calculus	_____	lith/o
eat	_____	phag/o
uvula or staphylococcus	_____	staphyl/o
ear	_____	ot/o
breathe	_____	pne/o
cranium (skull)	_____	crani/o
bladder	_____	cyst/o
softening	_____	malac/o

Should you rework previous Review Sheets?

WORD PART	MEANING
neur/o	_____ nerve
blast/o	_____ embryonic form
angi/o	_____ vessel
spasm	_____ spasm
scler/o	_____ hard
my/o	_____ muscle
fibr/o	_____ fibrous–fiber
lys/o	_____ destruction
lip/o	_____ fat
cyt/o	_____ cell
hem/o	_____ blood
hemat/o	_____ blood
arthr/o	_____ joint
phob/o	_____ fear
spermat/o	_____ spermatozoa
cyst/o	_____ bladder
o/o	_____ ovum
gen/o	_____ origin, beginning
oophor/o	_____ ovary
pex/o /y	_____ fixation
salping/o	_____ fallopian tube
hyster/o	_____ uterus
cele	_____ herniation
ptosis	_____ prolapse
path/o	_____ disease

REVIEW SHEET NO. 9

MEANING	WORD PART	
fear	_____	phob/o
vessel	_____	angi/o
uterus	_____	hyster/o
destruction	_____	lys/o
origin, beginning	_____	gen/o
blood	_____	hemat/o–hem/o
blood	_____	hem/o–hemat/o
bladder	_____	cyst/o
hard	_____	scler/o
joint	_____	arthr/o
fallopian tube	_____	salping/o
muscle	_____	my/o
nerve	_____	neur/o
fixation	_____	pex/o /y
cell	_____	cyt/o
embryonic form	_____	blast/o
ovary	_____	oophor/o
herniation	_____	cele
disease	_____	path/o
ovum	_____	o/o
prolapse	_____	ptosis
fat	_____	lip/o
spermatozoa	_____	spermat/o
fibrous–fiber	_____	fibr/o
spasm	_____	spasm

Should you rework previous Review Sheets?

WORD PART	MEANING	
blephar/o	_____	eyelid
nephr/o	_____	kidney
lith/o	_____	stone, calculus
pyel/o	_____	renal pelvis
plast/o /y	_____	repair
ureter/o	_____	ureter
ostomy	_____	new opening
orrhaphy	_____	suture
urethr/o	_____	urethra
otomy	_____	incision
ectomy	_____	excision
cyst/o	_____	bladder
cyt/o	_____	cell
orrhagia	_____	hemorrhage
orrhea	_____	flow
pneumon/o	_____	lung
pneum/o	_____	air
pne/o	_____	breathing
melan/o	_____	black
myc/o	_____	fungus
carcin/o	_____	cancer
rhin/o	_____	nose
thorac/o	_____	thorax or chest
meter, metr/o	_____	measure

REVIEW SHEET NO. 11

MEANING	WORD PART	
hemorrhage	_____	orrhagia
cell	_____	cyt/o
renal pelvis	_____	pyel/o
measure	_____	meter–metr/o
black	_____	melan/o
ureter	_____	ureter/o
excision	_____	ectomy
kidney	_____	nephr/o
cancer	_____	carcin/o
lung	_____	pneumon/o
urethra	_____	urethr/o
thorax or chest	_____	thorac/o
air	_____	pneum/o
suture	_____	orrhaphy
nose	_____	rhin/o
fungus	_____	myc/o
breathing	_____	pne/o
flow	_____	orrhea
bladder	_____	cyst/o
incision	_____	otomy
new opening	_____	ostomy
repair	_____	plast/o /y
stone, calculus	_____	lith/o
eyelid	_____	blephar/o

Should you rework previous Review Sheets?

WORD PART	MEANING	
stomat/o	_____	mouth
dent/o	_____	tooth
gloss/o	_____	tongue
cheil/o	_____	lip
gingiv/o	_____	gum
esophag/o	_____	esophagus
gastr/o	_____	stomach
enter/o	_____	small intestine
duoden/o	_____	duodenum
col/o	_____	colon
rect/o	_____	rectum
proct/o	_____	anus or rectum
hepat/o	_____	liver
pancreat/o	_____	pancreas
clys/o,-clys/is	_____	wash–irrigate
ectas/ia, ectas/is	_____	dilatation–stretch
scop/o	_____	examination
arteri/o	_____	artery
pleg/a /ia /ic	_____	paralysis
phleb/o	_____	vein
pex/o	_____	fixation
hyster/o	_____	uterus
orrhea	_____	flow
orrhaphy	_____	suture
cyst/o	_____	bladder

REVIEW SHEET NO. 13

MEANING	WORD PART
paralysis	pleg/a
	/ia
	/ic
duodenum	duoden/o
liver	hepat/o
suture	orrhaphy
small intestine	enter/o
tooth	dent/o
flow	orrhea
artery	arteri/o
anus or rectum	proct/o
lip	cheil/o
wash–irrigate	clys/is–clys/o
esophagus	esophag/o
uterus	hyster/o
bladder	cyst/o
fixation	pex/o
examination	scop/o
colon	col/o
gum	gingiv/o
mouth	stomat/o
vein	phleb/o
dilatation–stretch	ectas/ia
	/is
pancreas	pancreat/o
rectum	rect/o
tongue	gloss/o
stomach	gastr/o

Should you rework previous Review Sheets?

REVIEW SHEET NO. 14

WORD PART	MEANING
orrhexis	_____	rupture
orrhaphy	_____	suture
orrhea	_____	flow
orrhagia	_____	hemorrhage
esthesi/o	_____	feeling-sensation
an–a	_____	without
log/o	_____	study
dys	_____	bad, painful, difficult
hypo	_____	less than normal
par/a	_____	around–beyond
hyper	_____	more than normal
alges/i	_____	abnormal sensitivity
troph/o	_____	development
lys/o	_____	destruction
oste/o	_____	bone
arthr/o	_____	joint
phas/o	_____	speech
phon/o	_____	voice
tach/y	_____	fast
brad/y	_____	slow
my/o	_____	muscle
blast/o	_____	embryonic form
fibr/o	_____	fibrous, fiber
gram/o	_____	recording
gram	_____	the record
graph	_____	the instrument
graphy	_____	the process

REVIEW SHEET NO. 15

MEANING	WORD PART	
destruction	_____	lys/o
fast	_____	tach/y
flow	_____	orrhea
more than normal	_____	hyper
fibrous, fiber	_____	fibr/o
without	_____	an–a
bone	_____	oste/o
joint	_____	arthr/o
recording	_____	gram/o
the process	_____	graphy
the instrument	_____	graph
the record	_____	gram
bad, painful, difficult	_____	dys
rupture	_____	orrhexis
voice	_____	phon/o
muscle	_____	my/o
feeling–sensation	_____	esthesi/o
less than normal	_____	hypo
development	_____	troph/o
embryonic form	_____	blast/o
slow	_____	brad/y
suture	_____	orrhaphy
abnormal sensitivity	_____	alges/i
study	_____	log/o
around–beyond	_____	par/a
speech	_____	phas/o
hemorrhage	_____	orrhagia

Should you rework previous Review Sheets?

REVIEW SHEET NO. 16

WORD PART	MEANING	
dipl/o	_____	double
phon/o	_____	voice
opia	_____	vision
amb/i	_____	both
cocc/o	_____	coccus
cyan/o	_____	blue
neur/o	_____	nerve
tripsy	_____	surgical crushing
pyel/o	_____	renal pelvis
cyt/o	_____	cell
cyst/o	_____	bladder
cele	_____	herniation
dys	_____	bad, painful, difficult
chondr/o	_____	cartilage
cost/o	_____	rib
plas/o	_normal development_	formation, development
psych/o	_____	mind or soul
osis	_____	condition
oma	_____	tumor
oid	_____	resembling
pro	_____	before
gnos/o	_____	knowledge or know
di/a	_____	through
orrhea	_____	flow
orrhaphy	_____	suture
orrhagia	_____	hemorrhage
orrhexis	_____	rupture

troph o - r

REVIEW SHEET NO. 17

MEANING	WORD PART	
cell	_____	cyt/o
formation, development	_____	plas/o
double	_____	dipl/o
tumor	_____	oma
flow	_____	orrhea
blue	_____	cyan/o
herniation	_____	cele
condition	_____	osis
rupture	_____	orrhexis
coccus	_____	cocc/o
renal pelvis	_____	pyel/o
mind or soul	_____	psych/o
through	_____	di/a
rib	_____	cost/o
hemorrhage	_____	orrhagia
voice	_____	phon/o
surgical crushing	_____	trips/y
suture	_____	orrhaphy
resembling	_____	oid
both	_____	amb/i
cartilage	_____	chondr/o
before	_____	pro
vision	_____	opia
bad, painful, difficult	_____	dys
nerve	_____	neur/o
knowledge or know	_____	gnos/o
bladder	_____	cyst/o

REVIEW SHEET NO. 18

WORD PART	MEANING	
therm/o	_____	heat
esthesi/o	_____	feeling
metr/o, meter	_____	measure
phob/o	_____	fear
pleg/a	_____	paralysis
scop/o	_____	examine
micr/o	_____	small
macr/o	_____	large
cephal/o	_____	head
myel/o	_____	bone marrow
ot/o	_____	ear
rhin/o	_____	nose
cheil/o	_____	lip
dactyl/o	_____	finger or toe
megal/o	_____	enlargement
pol/y	_____	many
ur/o	_____	urine
neur/o	_____	nerve
psych/o	_____	mind or soul
arthr/o	_____	joint
oste/o	_____	bone
syn	_____	with
drom/o	_____	running with (symptom)
ectas/ia /is	_____	dilatation

REVIEW SHEET NO. 19

MEANING	WORD PART	
bone marrow	_____	myel/o
measure	_____	metr/o, meter
mind or soul	_____	psych/o
nose	_____	rhin/o
paralysis	_____	pleg/a
large	_____	macr/o
with	_____	syn
heat	_____	therm/o
finger or toe	_____	dactyl/o
urine	_____	ur/o
examine	_____	scop/o
symptom	_____	drom/o
enlargement	_____	megal/o
bone	_____	oste/o
many	_____	pol/y
ear	_____	ot/o
joint	_____	arthr/o
feeling	_____	esthesi/o
small	_____	micr/o
nerve	_____	neur/o
lip	_____	cheil/o
head	_____	cephal/o
fear	_____	phob/o
dilatation	_____	ectas/ia /is

Should you rework previous Review Sheets?

REVIEW SHEET NO. 20

WORD PART		MEANING
dips/o	_____	thirst, drink
pol/y	_____	many
mania	_____	madness
anter/o	_____	before
poster/o	_____	behind, after
dors/o	_____	back
ventr/o	_____	belly
cephal/o	_____	head
encephal/o	_____	brain
aer/o	_____	air
chrom/o	_____	color
lys/o	_____	destruction
metr/o meter	_____	measure
gen/o ic esis ous	_____	beginning-formation *origin*
phil/o	_____	attraction
eu	_____	good
peps/ia	_____	digestion
kinesi/o	_____	movement
men/o	_____	menses–menstruation
stasis	_____	halt–control
syphil/o	_____	syphilis
pseud/o	_____	false
edema	_____	swelling
opia	_____	vision
ptosis	_____	prolapse

REVIEW SHEET NO. 21

MEANING	WORD PART	
back	_____	dors/o
attraction	_____	phil/o
vision	_____	opia
madness	_____	mania
destruction	_____	lys/o
menses–menstruation	_____	men/o
swelling	_____	edema
measure	_____	metr/o, meter
thirst, drink	_____	dips/o
brain	_____	encephal/o
digestion	_____	peps/ia
syphilis	_____	syphil/o
prolapse	_____	ptosis
air	_____	aer/o
belly	_____	ventr/o
before	_____	anter/o
many	_____	pol/y
false	_____	pseud/o
halt–control	_____	stasis
movement	_____	kinesi/o
good	_____	eu
beginning–~~formation~~ *again*	_____	gen/o ic esis ous
color	_____	chrom/o
head	_____	cephal/o
behind–after	_____	poster/o

Should you rework previous Review Sheets?

REVIEW SHEET NO. 22

WORD PART	MEANING	
lapar/o	_____	abdominal wall
hepat/o	_____	liver
col/o	_____	colon
bi/o	_____	life
pyr/o	_____	fever, fire
xanth/o	_____	yellow
chlor/o	_____	green
opia	_____	vision
erythr/o	_____	red
leuk/o	_____	white
melan/o	_____	black
cyt/o	_____	cell
cyst/o	_____	bladder
derm/o	_____	skin
blast/o	_____	embryonic form
emia	_____	blood
hidr/o	_____	sweat
aden/o	_____	gland
gynec/o	_____	woman
path/o	_____	disease
plast/o	_____	repair
ophthalm/o	_____	eye
viscer/o	_____	organ
glyc/o	_____	sugar
hypo	_____	less than normal
later/o	_____	side

erathro (handwritten note next to erythr/o)

REVIEW SHEET NO. 23

MEANING	WORD PART	
gland	_____	aden/o
skin	_____	derm/o
white	_____	leuk/o
yellow	_____	xanth/o
disease	_____	path/o
bladder	_____	cyst/o
side	_____	later/o
organ	_____	viscer/o
sweat	_____	hidr/o
abdominal wall	_____	lapar/o
eye	_____	ophthalm/o
fever, fire	_____	pyr/o
less than normal	_____	hypo
embryonic form	_____	blast/o
liver	_____	hepat/o
woman	_____	gynec/o
black	_____	melan/o
sugar	_____	glyc/o
life	_____	bi/o
red	_____	erythr/o
blood	_____	emia
repair	_____	plast/o
colon	_____	col/o
green	_____	chlor/o
vision	_____	opia

Should you rework previous Review Sheets?

REVIEW SHEET NO. 24

WORD PART	MEANING	
orchid/o	_____	testes, testicles
pex/o	_____	fixation
crypt/o	_____	hidden
colp/o	_____	vagina
dyn/o /ia	_____	pain
spasm	_____	spasm
orrhaphy	_____	suture
orrhea	_____	flow
orrhagia	_____	hemorrhage
orrhexis	_____	rupture
end/o	_____	inner
mes/o	_____	middle
ect/o	_____	outer
hyster/o	_____	uterus
ectop/o	_____	misplaced
retr/o	_____	behind–backward
par/a	_____	around
hepat/o	_____	liver
aut/o	_____	self
hem/o	_____	blood
py/o	_____	pus
muc/o	_____	mucus
mon/o	_____	single
mult/i	_____	many
lip/o	_____	fat
ectas/ia /is	_____	dilatation

REVIEW SHEET NO. 25

MEANING	WORD PART	
outer–outside	_____	ect/o
pain	_____	dyn/o /ia
rupture	_____	orrhexis
many	_____	mult/i
testes, testicles	_____	orchid/o
inner	_____	end/o
mucus	_____	muc/o
flow	_____	orrhea
behind–backward	_____	retr/o
fat	_____	lip/o
fixation	_____	pex/o
blood	_____	hem/o
dilatation	_____	ectas/ia /is
middle	_____	mes/o
suture	_____	orrhaphy
single	_____	mon/o
uterus	_____	hyster/o
around	_____	par/a
hidden	_____	crypt/o
pus	_____	py/o
liver	_____	hepat/o
misplaced	_____	ectop/o
vagina	_____	colp/o
hemorrhage	_____	orrhagia
spasm	_____	spasm

Should you rework previous Review Sheets?

REVIEW SHEET NO. 26

WORD PART	MEANING	
null/i	_____	none
ab	_____	from
ad	_____	toward
de	_____	from
ex	_____	from
narc/o	_____	sleep
leps/o	_____	seizure
is/o	_____	equal
anis/o	_____	unequal
dactyl/o	_____	fingers–toes
peri	_____	around
chondr/o	_____	cartilage
cost/o	_____	rib
aden/o	_____	gland
circum	_____	around
di/a	_____	through
per	_____	through
necr/o	_____	dead
ectomy	_____	excision
otomy	_____	incision
phob/o	_____	fear
phil/o	_____	attraction
ectop/o	_____	misplaced
phag/o	_____	eat

MEANING	WORD PART	
cartilage	_____	chondr/o
sleep	_____	narc/o
fingers–toes	_____	dactyl/o
attraction	_____	phil/o
from	_____	de–ab–ex
from	_____	ab–de–ex
from	_____	ex–ab–de
incision	_____	otomy
rib	_____	cost/o
toward	_____	ad
excision	_____	ectomy
fear	_____	phob/o
none	_____	null/i
seizure	_____	leps/o
dead	_____	necr/o
equal	_____	is/o
gland	_____	aden/o
through	_____	per–di/a
through	_____	di/a–per
misplaced	_____	ectop/o
unequal	_____	anis/o
around	_____	circum–peri
around	_____	peri–circum
eat	_____	phag/o

Should you rework previous Review Sheets?

WORD PART	MEANING	
hom/o	_____	same
heter/o	_____	different
lys/o	_____	destruction
pex/o	_____	fixation
sym	_____	together
super	_____	above
pub/o	_____	pubis
supra	_____	above
par/o	_____	bear
syn	_____	together
metr/o, hyster/o	_____	uterus
orrhexis	_____	rupture
orrhaphy	_____	suture
salping/o	_____	fallopian tube
oophor/o	_____	ovary
epi	_____	over–upon
extra	_____	in addition to–beyond
infra	_____	below–under
sub	_____	under–below
sept/o	_____	infection
phag/o	_____	eat
anti	_____	against
contra	_____	against
trans	_____	across–over
trips/y	_____	crushing
ectop/o	_____	misplaced

REVIEW SHEET NO. 29

MEANING	WORD PART	
rupture	_____	orrhexis
in addition to–beyond	_____	extra
above	_____	super–supra
above	_____	supra–super
together	_____	syn–sym
together	_____	sym–syn
fallopian tube	_____	salping/o
misplaced	_____	ectop/o
against	_____	contra–anti
against	_____	anti–contra
fixation	_____	pex/o
different	_____	heter/o
across–over	_____	trans
ovary	_____	oophor/o
pubis	_____	pub/o
infection	_____	sept/o
suture	_____	orrhaphy
destruction	_____	lys/o
eat	_____	phag/o
crushing	_____	trips/y
same	_____	hom/o
bear	_____	par/o
under–below	_____	sub–infra
below–under	_____	infra–sub
over–upon	_____	epi
uterus	_____	hyster/o, metr/o

Should you rework previous Review Sheets?

REVIEW SHEET NO. 30

WORD PART	MEANING	
tri	_____	three
bi	_____	two–double
semi	_____	half
hemi	_____	half
troph/o	_____	development
con	_____	with
dis	_____	to free–to undo
post	_____	after, behind
pre	_____	before, in front of
intr/a	_____	within
cervic/o	_____	neck of uterus–neck
nas/o	_____	nose
pharyng/o	_____	pharynx
laryng/o	_____	larynx
trache/o	_____	trachea
bronch/o	_____	bronchus
pleur/o	_____	pleura
centesis	_____	puncture
sinistr/o	_____	left
dextr/o	_____	right
vas/o	_____	vessel
ne/o	_____	new
penia	_____	lack of
splen/o	_____	spleen
uni	_____	one

MEANING	WORD PART	
nose	_____	nas/o
pleura	_____	pleur/o
with	_____	con
before, in front of	_____	pre
lack of	_____	penia
one	_____	uni
larynx	_____	laryng/o
half	_____	hemi–semi
half	_____	semi–hemi
to free–to undo	_____	dis
right	_____	dextr/o
bronchus	_____	bronch/o
vessel	_____	vas/o
two–double	_____	bi
puncture	_____	centesis
within	_____	intr/a
spleen	_____	splen/o
three	_____	tri
left	_____	sinistr/o
trachea	_____	trache/o
new	_____	ne/o
pharynx	_____	pharyng/o
neck of uterus, neck	_____	cervic/o
after, behind	_____	post
development	_____	troph/o

Should you rework previous Review Sheets?

REVIEW SHEET NO. 32

WORD PART	MEANING	
noct/i	_____	night
nyct/o	_____	night
opia	_____	vision
ankyl/o	_____	stiff
phor/o	_____	bear–carry
eu	_____	good, well, easy
stasis	_____	stopping, controlling
calcane/o	_____	heel
pharyng/o	_____	pharynx
carp/o	_____	wrist
schiz/o, schist/o, or schisis	_____	split
hist/o	_____	tissue
ischi/o	_____	ischium *bone you sit*
stern/o	_____	sternum
phalang/o	_____	phalanges
acromi/o	_____	acromion
humer/o	_____	humerus
condyl/o	_____	condyle
gangli/o	_____	ganglia
thromb/o	_____	clot, thrombus
trich/o	_____	hair
orrhexis	_____	rupture
ectop/o	_____	misplaced
ante	_____	before, forward
plasm/o	_____	formation

REVIEW SHEET NO. 33

MEANING	WORD PART	
split	_____	schisis, schist/o, or schiz/o
bear, carry	_____	phor/o
night	_____	nyct/o–noct/i
night	_____	noct/i–nyct/o
before, forward	_____	ante
wrist	_____	carp/o
formation	_____	plasm/o, plas/o, troph/o, gen/o
clot, thrombus	_____	thromb/o
stopping, controlling	_____	stasis
hair	_____	trich/o
humerus	_____	humer/o
heel	_____	calcane/o
misplaced	_____	ectop/o
sternum	_____	stern/o
rupture	_____	orrhexis
ganglia	_____	gangli/o
ischium	_____	ischi/o
vision	_____	opia
condyle	_____	condyl/o
tissue	_____	hist/o
acromion	_____	acromi/o
pharynx	_____	pharyng/o
good, well, easy	_____	eu
phalanges	_____	phalang/o
stiff	_____	ankyl/o

Should you rework previous Review Sheets?

REVIEW SHEET NO. 34

WORD PART	MEANING	
corne/o	_____	cornea
scler/o	_____	sclera
ir/o	_____	iris
irid/o	_____	iris
retin/o	_____	retina
cor/e, core/o	_____	pupil
kerat/o	_____	cornea
cycl/o	_____	ciliary body
pleg/a	_____	paralysis
lacrim/o	_____	tear
dacry/o	_____	tear
tome	_____	instrument for incising
tympan/o	_____	eardrum
ren/o	_____	kidney
vesic/o	_____	bladder
pod/o	_____	foot
chir/o	_____	hands
crypt/o	_____	hidden
emia	_____	blood
rachi/o, rach/i	_____	spine
omphal/o	_____	navel
onych/o	_____	nail
phren/o	_____	diaphragm
om/o	_____	shoulder
myx/o	_____	mucus

REVIEW SHEET NO. 35

MEANING	WORD PART	
bladder	_____	vesic/o
cornea	_____	kerat/o–corne/o
cornea	_____	corne/o–kerat/o
blood	_____	emia
mucus	_____	myx/o–muc/o
instrument for incising	_____	tome
iris	_____	ir/o–irid/o
iris	_____	irid/o–ir/o
diaphragm	_____	phren/o
retina	_____	retin/o
tear	_____	dacry/o–lacrim/o
tear	_____	lacrim/o–dacry/o
nail	_____	onych/o
hands	_____	chir/o
eardrum	_____	tympan/o
shoulder	_____	om/o
navel	_____	omphal/o
ciliary body	_____	cycl/o
sclera	_____	scler/o
foot	_____	pod/o
spine	_____	rachi/o, rach/i
hidden	_____	crypt/o
kidney	_____	ren/o
pupil	_____	cor/e, core/o
paralysis	_____	pleg/a

You can rework Review Sheets anytime.

APPENDIX B

Glossary of Word Parts Learned

WORD PART	INTRODUCED IN FRAME NUMBER	WORD PART	INTRODUCED IN FRAME NUMBER
a	532	cephal/o	276
ab	344	cerebr/o	430
abdomin/o	363	cervic/o	1267
acr/o	91	cheil/o	675
acromi/o	1383	chir/o	1468
ad	355	chlor/o	906
aden/o	231	chol/e	495
aer/o	854	chondr/o	320
alges/i	727	chrom/o	866
algia	174	circum	1067
amb/i	750	clys/o	685
an	724	cocc/o	449
angi/o	550	col/o	688
anis/o	1056	colp/o	962
ankyl/o	1332	con	1217
ante	1234	condyl/o	1389
anter/o	848	contra	1164
anti	1158	cor/e, core/o	1430
appendic/o	1260	corne/o	1412
arteri/o	555	cortic/o	1261
arthr/o	309	cost/o	325
aut/o	994	crani/o	423
bi	1201	crypt/o	956
bi/o	856	cyan/o	109
blast/o	550	cycl/o	1438
blephar/o	608	cyst/o	370
brad/y	507	cyt/o	137
bronch/o	1271	dacry/o	1448
calcane/o	1355	dactyl/o	808
carcin/o	245	de	1022
cardi/o	150	dent/o	336
carp/o	1360	derm/o	129
caud/o	840	dermat/o	103
cele	290	dextr/o	1299
centesis	365	di/a	788

283

WORD PART	INTRODUCED IN FRAME NUMBER	WORD PART	INTRODUCED IN FRAME NUMBER
dipl/o	745	hist/o	1309
dips/o	829	hom/o	1098
dis	1227	humer/o	1385
dors/o	836	hydr/o	385
drom/o	822	hyper	216
duoden/o	183	hypo	224
dyn/o	279	hyster/o	597
dys	541	in	1181
ect/o	969	infra	1143
ectas/ia, ectas/is	683	inter	331
ectomy	178	intr/a	1241
ectop/o	982	ir/o	1414
edema	892	irid/o	1422
electr/o	169	is/o	1050
emesis	218	ischi/o	1366
emia	910	itis	108
encephal/o	288	kerat/o	1435
end/o	967	kinesi/o	511
enter/o	683	lacrim/o	1442
epi	1133	lapar/o	898
erythr/o	906	laryng/o	262
esophag/o	709	later/o	848
esthesi/o	724	leps/o	1046
eu	872	leuk/o	132
ex	1034	lip/o	242
external	849	lith/o	491
extra	1138	log/o	166
femor/o	1373	lumb/o	397
fibr/o	553	lymph/o	886
gangli/o	1392	lys/o	554
gastr/o	155	macr/o	804
gen/o	470	mal	1193
gingiv/o	679	malac/o	295
gloss/o	670	mania	159
glyc/o	944	medi/o	848
gnos/o	783	megal/o	97
gram/o	170	melan/o	641
graph/o	171	men/o	881
gynec/o	917	mening/o	443
hem/o	559	mes/o	968
hemat/o	560	metr/o, meter	419
hemi	1212	metr/o (uterus)	1126
hepat/o	701	micr/o	800
heter/o	1103	mon/o	1000
hidr/o	912	muc/o	252

WORD PART	INTRODUCED IN FRAME NUMBER	WORD PART	INTRODUCED IN FRAME NUMBER
mult/i	1004	phalang/o	1380
my/o	738	pharyng/o	1271
myc/o	650	phas/o	733
myel/o	764	phil/o	1092
myx/o	1528	phleb/o	713
narc/o	1041	phob/o	390
nas/o	1271	phon/o	735
necr/o	1084	phor/o	1338
ne/o	1313	phren/o	1524
nephr/o	612	plas/o	767
neur/o	550	plasm/o	1314
noct/i	1319	plast/o	312
nyct/o	1324	pleg/a	1425
null/i	1012	pleur/o	1271
o/o	568	pne/o	525
oid	249	pneum/o	656
om/o	1527	pneumon/o	635
oma	235	pod/o	1467
omphal/o	1511	pol/y	811
onych/o	1517	post	1232
oophor/o	572	poster/o	841
ophthalm/o	920	pre	1233
opia	747	pro	785
orchid/o	953	proct/o	697
orrhagia	632	pseud/o	890
orrhaphy	625	psych/o	772
orrhea	473	ptosis	603
orrhexis	717	pub/o	404
osis	115	py/o	464
oste/o	301	pyel/o	619
ostomy	185	pyr/o	902
ot/o	477	rach/i, rachi/o	1504
otomy	191	rect/o	692
pancreat/o	704	ren/o	1466
par/a	730	retin/o	1427
paralysis	117	retr/o	986
par/o	1008	rhin/o	484
path/o	238	salping/o	581
pelv/i	412	sanguin/o	1223
penia	142	scapul/o	1382
peps/o	544	schiz/o	1349
per	1077	scler/o	552
peri	1063	scop/o	664
pex/o	577	semi	1212
phag/o	508	sept/o	1153

WORD PART	INTRODUCED IN FRAME NUMBER	WORD PART	INTRODUCED IN FRAME NUMBER
sinistr/o	1294	thromb/o	1398
spasm	551	tome	125
spermat/o	562	trache/o	1271
spir/o	1179	trans	1171
splen/o	1108	tri	1199
staphyl/o	455	trich/o	1405
stasis	884	trips/y	761
stern/o	1375	troph/o	221
stomat/o	664	tympan/o	1464
strept/o	453	uni	1199
sub	1146	ur/o	616
super	848	ureter/o	622
sym	1112	urethr/o	629
syn	816	vas/o	1303
syphil/o	887	ventr/o	843
tach/y	520	vesic/o	1465
therap/o	661	viscer/o	894
therm/o	794	xanth/o	906
thorac/o	377		

APPENDIX C

Additional Word Parts

Following are some word parts that you can use with your word-building system. (There are others, of course, but these build fairly important and useful words.) If you want to enlarge your vocabulary dramatically:

1. pick a word part that interests you,
2. look for it in your dictionary,
3. note how many words begin with this part,
4. list five of them with their meanings.

Other words that contain the word part you worked with exist; for example, **therm**/o/meter and hyper/**therm**/ia.

WORD PART	MEANING	EXAMPLE
actin/o	ray	actin/o/dermat/itis
all/o	other, different	all/o/plas/ia
ambl/y	dim, dull	ambl/y/op/ia
andr/o	man, male	andr/o/path/y
antr/o	cavity, antrum	antr/o/scop/y
atel/o	incomplete, imperfect	atel/o/gloss/ia
audi/o	hear, hearing	audi/o/meter
balan/o	glans (penis or clitoris)	balan/o/plast/y
bar/o	weight, heavy	hyp/o/bar/o/path/y
bil/i	bile	bil/i/ur/ia
cac/o	bad, diseased, abnormal	cac/o/rhin/ia
cari/o	decay	cari/o/gen/ic
cat/a	down, downward	cat/a/leps/y
celi/o	abdominal region	celi/o/my/algia
chron/o	time	chron/ic
clas/ia	breaking	arthr/o/clas/ia
cleis/is	closure, occlusion	colp/o/cleis/is
coll/o	glutinous, jellylike	coll/oid
copr/o	feces, excrement	copr/o/stas/is
cry/o	cold, freezing	cry/o/therap/y
doch/o	duct	chol/e/doch/itis

287

WORD PART	MEANING	EXAMPLE
epipl/o	omentum	epipl/o/pex/y
episi/o	vulva	episi/otomy
erg/o	work	syn/erg/y
es/o	within, inward	es/o/phor/ia
febr/i	fever	febr/ile
gli/o	glue, neuroglia	gli/oma
gnath/o	jaw	pro/gnath/ia
hyal/o	glassy, transparent	hyal/o/muc/oid
ichthy/o	fish	ichthy/osis
idi/o	personal, one's own	idi/o/path/y
in/o	fiber, fibrous	in/o/cyst/oma
kerat/o	horny, cornea	kerat/o/dermat/itis
labi/o	lip	labi/o/myc/osis
lal/o	speech disorder	ech/o/lal/ia
lept/o	thin, light, slender	lept/o/mening/itis
mel/o	limb	hem/i/mel/ia
met/a	after, change	met/a/stas/is
morph/o	form	morph/o/log/y
myring/o	ear drum	myc/o/myring/itis
nev/o	birthmark, mole	nev/o/carcin/oma
ocul/o	eye	ocul/o/nas/al
odont/o	tooth	odont/o/blast
olig/o	few, little, scant	olig/o/phren/ia
onc/o	tumor, mass	onc/o/lys/is

opt/o
  optic/o
	vision	opt/o/meter
		  optic/ian

orth/o	correct, straight	orth/o/scop/ic
osm/o	odor, sense of smell	an/osm/ia
ox/y	sharp, acute, acid	ox/y/cephal/y
pach/y	thick	pach/y/blephar/osis
papill/o	nipple-like, papilla	pappil/o/retin/itis
perine/o	perineum	perine/orrhaphy
phac/o phak/o	lens of the eye	phac/oid phak/o/cele
phall/o	penis	phall/ic
phot/o	light	phot/o/therap/y
phyt/o	plant	dermat/o/phyt/osis
pil/o	hair	pil/o/cyst/ic
plat/y	flat, broad	plat/y/cran/ia
plic/i	fold	plic/a
poli/o	gray	poli/o/myel/itis
prot/o	first	prot/o/plasm
pteryg/o	wing	pteryg/oid
radicul/o	root	radicul/o/neur/itis
sarc/o	flesh	sarc/oma
scoli/o	curved, curvature	scoli/osis

WORD PART	MEANING	EXAMPLE
scot/o	darkness	scot/oma
seb/o	sebum	seb/orrhea
sial/o	saliva	sial/o/aden/itis
sit/o	food	sit/o/therap/y
somat/o	body	psych/o/somat/ic
somn/o /i	sleep	in/somn/ia
sphygm/o	pulse	sphygm/o/man/o/meter
spondyl/o	vertebra	spondyl/o/lys/is
sten/o	narrowness, constriction	sten/osis
stere/o	solid, solid body	stere/o/gnos/is
steth/o	chest	steth/o/scop/e
sthen/o	strength	a/sthen/ia
stigmat/o	mark, point	a/stigmat/ism
tel/e	distant, far	tel/e/metr/y
terat/o	monster, wonder	terat/oma
tetr/a	four	tetr/a/log/y
thant/o	death	thant/oid
trop/o	turning	heter/o/trop/ia
varic/o	varicose vein	varic/o/cele
ven/o	vein, vena cava	ven/o/clys/is
xen/o	strange, foreign	xen/o/phob/ia
xer/o	dry	xer/o/derm/a